Trouble is My Middle Name

Reg Jarvis

Edward Gaskell publishers
DEVON

First Published 2007 by
Edward Gaskell *Publishers*
The Old Sawmill
Grange Road
Bideford • Devon
EX39 4AS

ISBN 10: 1-898546-93-2
ISBN 13: 978-1-898546-93-1

Cover photograph by Lesley Horton-Bennett

Trouble is My Middle Name

Reg Jarvis

Printed and Bound by
Lazarus Press
Unit 7 Caddsdown Business Park
Bideford
Devon
EX39 3DX

Trouble is My Middle Name

Reg Jarvis

For my family

Contents

Foreword

When the poet laureate William Wordsworth wrote these beautiful words:

> *'. . . that best portion of a good man's life: his little, nameless, unre-membered acts of kindness and love. . .'*

it is as if they were written in honour of my dear friend Reg Jarvis.

Reg has been a friend of my wife, Val, for 40 years and I have had the privilege of knowing him for over 25. We have both admired his many achievements and consider ourselves fortunate that we were able to spend time with him in Ireland, when he lived at Kilmore Quay, witnessing at first hand the regard in which he was held by all in that beautiful village.

Reg has always been highly respected by his colleagues and now the fulfilling life he has led is recorded for his family and descendants.

It is an honour to have known him and shared his friendship, which Val and I will always cherish.

Cllr. Andrew Eastman
Mayor of Northam, Devon
1st November 2007

Chapter One

CHILDHOOD

The 29th January 1926 was a cold blustery morning with a thin covering of snow on the roofs of the houses. My mother, Lilly Jarvis, was in bed in the delivery ward of the nursing home in Abbey Wood, North East London. The nursing sister approached the bed and said, "come on Lillian it's time your baby came forth, drink this."

"What is it sister?" my mother asked.

"Quinine," was the answer.

"But I can't have quinine sister, I am allergic to it."

"Never mind about that my girl, it is time that we encouraged your little mite to come into the world." Whereupon the sister put the cup to my mother's mouth and poured the liquid down her throat.

Some time later a nurse came to my mother and found that her face was swollen and very red. My mother screamed that the baby was coming. The nurse quickly fetched the sister and as soon as my head came into sight the sister saw that I was a strange colour. As I gradually came into the world the sister could see that I was a light blue, and I was rushed into the intensive care ward.

The quinine had affected the oxygen supply from my mother's system to my body. After oxygen and blood transfusions, I was brought round, but it was not possible for me to be breast-fed in case my mother's milk was affected. So, I became a 'Cow and Gate' baby which meant an extra expense for my parents.

My father, who was 27 at the time, had served in the Royal Naval Air Service which was the forerunner of the Royal Air Force. He lived under canvas, spending his days servicing the by-planes in Norfolk. Before the war he had qualified at the London School of Arts and Crafts as a tinsmith and silversmith. As full time jobs were difficult to get after the war he made petrol tanks for the Matchless Motorcycle Company and in addition made dustpans and crumb trays for Gamages of Holborn, but because both these companies wanted credit from their suppliers, money was very short. My father, like so many others, was under-capitalised.

It was because of this that, during my early days, my parents were seeking another way of earning more money. My mother's two sisters, Elizabeth and Milly, both lived in Rugby in Warwickshire, and their husbands both worked at the British Thomson Houston Company, an engineering company, which made turbines and electrical apparatus. Elizabeth's husband had been a blacksmith in Scotland and then in Durham before he joined the B.T.H. in the foundry department. Milly's husband George had joined the management team as a training officer. The B.T.H. engineering company was a very forward looking company. It was George who persuaded my father to consider moving to Rugby to join the tinsmith department at a salary of £4.50 a week.

I remember my journey to Rugby at the tender age of three. My father had a Matchless motor bike and he had built himself a side-car with special springing and a cover for wet weather. It was a long journey from Woolwich to Rugby and I remember my mother telling me, after many enquiries from me of 'are we there yet?' Saying "no, when you see the wireless masts we won't be long." I kept looking out of the windscreen and before long saw some high masts in a field we were passing and asked if they were the ones, but was told that they were the Daventry short wave masts. We were looking for the Hillmorton Radio Station and after a further half hour these masts came into sight. We soon came to Rugby where my uncle had obtained rooms to rent in what was known as

Lower Rugby near the factories and cattle market which held a fascination for me.

We had not lived here for very long when I caught scarlet fever which was very contagious. I was sent to an isolation hospital some miles from Rugby. My parents used to visit me on the motorbike but all they could do was wave at me through the window because the public were not allowed into the wards.

One night I wet my bed and the nurses were very cross with me because it meant a complete change of bed linen. They sat me on a table in the middle of the ward in my night dress whilst they changed the bed. As a result I caught a chill on top of the fever and I was what they called 'on the danger list' for a week. It was uncertain whether I would survive.

I did get better after a few weeks and was pronounced clear of the disease.

Meanwhile my father had settled into work as a tinsmith and was contemplating the purchase of his own house.

There was a new estate being built on the outskirts of the town to be called Hillmorton Paddox. I believe the price was £250 with a deposit of £50. We went to see these houses and took an option on an inside house. The area was very nice so when the building had been completed we bought the house and moved into number 69 Vernon Avenue.

From my perspective everything looked very big, as it does when you are only four years old. Even the grass in the garden was above my head as it had not been cut. The houses were built in blocks of four. The gardens of the outside houses were fifteen feet shorter than the middle two so that there was a back entrance to the centre two houses down an entry running by the side of the outside houses.

It was a dream house for the period and we had some very nice neighbours. As the estate developed, friends were made and by the time I started school I had made friends with a boy called Peter, who was two years older than me, and he took care of me. He lived at number 47, about 10 houses away from me. We grew up together and had similar hobbies. As I grew up, cycling became the major transport and there were many country lanes to explore.

Chapter Two

TEENS

In order to help with furnishing the house, my mother took in a lodger. Mr Usher was a very nice draughtsman from the B.T.H. on a training course. I got on very well with him and when he left us he gave me a model yacht that had been his father's before him. It was a lovely model, hand-made with a self-weighted rudder. My father made me polish it with Mansion Polish after I sailed it to keep it watertight.

I took it on a visit to my grandparents who lived in Bexleyheath, Kent because there was a park near them called Danson Park which had a large lake for sailing. One day I was sailing my model yacht when the wind took my boat right across the other side of the lake. I went around the edge to retrieve the boat and lost my way back to where my parents were picnicking. While running through the woods I lost the rudder from my boat, and I was devastated. Fortunately my uncle, who was a lot younger than my father, had a model railway layout and he suggested that he could make a rudder for me out of plywood and a melted railway wheel. So we found a piece of deal about $3/8''$ thick and drilled out a $1/2''$ hole and melted down a lead wheel and poured it into the hole in the rudder, screwed two hooks into the rudder and hooked it onto the boat. It was once more operational.

I was quite good at sport and used to play soccer at school. We had house teams; mine was Rockaby, and there was a lot of rivalry.

I was eleven and keen to be seen to be supporting my team so I took to tackling one of the bully boys (named Hope). He said he would kill me if I did not stop and of course I took no notice. One day he caught me by the bicycle sheds in the playground at the rear of the school. I was surrounded by his gang and he punched me several times, during which I must have hit my head against the corner of a brick wall. I went home that Wednesday and went to school on the Thursday because we were taking the eleven plus exams, but I had a bad headache and slept badly. I did not go to school on the Friday. On the Saturday, which was to be the Rag Week procession, my eyes would not focus. The doctor was called and after checking my eyes with a light and finding that my left arm was not responding to action, I was admitted to a private nursing home which fortunately had an up-to-date operating theatre. From notes that my father made, I was unconsious and near death. An ambulance was called and police cleared a way through the procession to get me to the nursing home.

My doctor was able to get the services of a specialist surgeon, who operated on my skull and removed a piece of bone the size of a half-a-crown from the right hand side of my brain. Unfortunately the bone had damaged the part of the brain which controlled my left side. I remained unconscious for three days and am told that my mother sat beside me all the while, even slept by my side at night. Apparently many people prayed for me from the Sunday School which I normally attended.

On the fourth day I woke up and asked why I was in my mother's bedroom because the wallpaper was like the paper she had in her room. This was the first sensible thing that I had said since the operation and meant that my brain and my eyes were working properly.

As I regained strength it was realised that I had become cross-eyed and had double vision. Each time the doctor came to see me he would hold up one finger and say "how many fingers am I holding up?" and I would see two. I was in bed for most of the summer but gradually my sight improved until I only saw one of an object held up.

It is difficult for most people to understand what it is like to be paralysed in an arm or leg. I had feeling in the flesh but could not feel anything a small distance away. It meant that I could not feel anything hot until it burnt me. I could move my arm but not my fingers. I could stand on my leg but not pick it up to move it. So I was taken out in a wheelchair and with only one side of my body functional I soon learnt I had to do things differently to other people. I had to learn to eat one-handed and dress likewise. My left arm was pulled up to remain on my chest as I grew and my hand was clasped and could not open. One thing I had to remember was that I must protect the right side of my head as there was a hole big enough to put my thumb in, although it was sealed with skin. I was told that if I had a knock on that side of my head I would be killed. This meant that although I could use the right side of my body, I had to protect the other side of my head.

My father made a hammock stand in the garden and I was carried out each fine day to be able to lie in the fresh air. This was very helpful in building up my strength. One day I was swinging in the hammock when I fell out. I struggled to get up and found that my left leg was strong enough to bear my weight but I could not move it. My mother was horrified when she came out into the garden but did not know whether to laugh or cry when she saw me standing up. I fell into her arms as I took my first step.

From then onwards it was trial and error until I learnt to swing my left leg round to move forward whilst balancing on my right leg. It was an entirely new way of walking but I soon found how to get around with sheer determination. It was surprising what could be done using only one side of the body. At eleven years old you can learn new ways of doing things surprisingly quickly.

My father found a poem entitled "It can be done" which has been my inspiration and is worth quoting here:

> Somebody said that it couldn't be done;
> So he, with a chuckle, replied
> That maybe it couldn't, but he would be one
> Who wouldn't say so till he tried.
>
> So he took off his coat, and he took off his hat,
> And the first thing we knew he'd begun it.
> He started to sing as he tackled
> What couldn't be done, and he did it

There are thousands to tell you it cannot be done,
There are thousands to prophesy failure
There are thousands to point out to you, one by one
The dangers that are bound to assail you.

But just buckle in, with a bit of a grin
Take off your coat and go to it
Just start to sing when you tackle the thing
That cannot be done, and you'll do it!

My father said that I had been trouble from the moment that I had been born. But I made great strides in recovery. There was an enquiry at the school but since there were three Hope boys, all of similar age at the school, and none of them owning up to any fight, there was little hope of finding out what had happened. The school board however awarded me a scholarship to the secondary school. I had reached a good standard in the examinations that I had taken so the authorities considered that the ones that I had missed would be the same.

People think that if one is paralysed one has no feeling in the limbs. This was not so with me since the paralysis was the result of damage to the control part of the brain, not the limbs themselves. Consequently I had a continual ache in my leg and arm as they grew. I therefore believed during my teens that I would only live until my early twenties. This just shows you that you should never give up since I am now in my eighties! Because I walked to school to exercise my leg, I developed quite a limp. I became well known along the main road and was frequently given lifts by other boys' parents. Schooling went very well for me and I was third in my class, but of course could do no sports or gym. I benefited from extra tutorials although I could not read for too long at a time because my eyes still suffered from a certain amount of double vision.

When asked what I wanted to do when I left school, I always had a yearning for farming, but was not strong enough to work on the land. I also liked science and biology and when I reached fifteen, the school leaving age at that time, I began to look around.

We were at that time subject to air-raids. Rugby was the start of the run in for the bombing of Coventry and Birmingham and we had very disturbed nights. My father was a fire-warden at night and a key worker by day. I well remember the Coventry blitz when wave after wave of German bombers dived over Coventry, 12 miles away, and the anti-aircraft guns rattled away to try to beat off the attack. Rugby for some reason did not get bombed very much in spite of having two large engineering companies manufacturing munitions..

My father and mother were both keen gardeners and they were looking forward to laying out the 100 foot garden which we had. It was decided to split the garden in half. The top part nearest to the house was to be a flower garden, landscaped with a pond. The lower half was to be vegetables (Dig For Victory). It was decided the Anderson air-raid shelter was to be in the middle of the garden, halfway from the house. Because of a high water level in the ground, the shelter could not be buried too deeply, so soil was thrown up over the shelter to camouflage it. This made a perfect rockery. My father made a pond in front of the rockery with a fountain and waterfall from the top of the shelter down to the pond.

He made a zinc tank on top of the shelter which would give a pressure for the fountain and made the pond overflow into a sunken barrel. He obtained a semi-rotary village pump with which we could pump the water from the barrel up to the zinc tank. Since the fountain was only small bore and the tank held about 50 gallons of water, it made quite an efficient process and stored water in case of fire. Between the pond and the house was a lawn which it was my job to cut each week. I also helped my father mixing concrete and we made paths around the lawn so that it could be mown up to the edge. We also made some steps from the French doors in the living room to the lawn and in the concrete my father put lead letters for the poem "One is nearer God's heart in a garden than anywhere else on earth." When these letters became dull one could scrape the feet over the letters and they would shine again.

My mother's time was taken up looking after me during my teens because I needed a lot of help dressing and preparing myself for school. She was well educated and helped me with my English, practising maths and drawing which I was very fond of. I had to think about most physical moves before putting them into action.

This made me appear very awkward but fortunately for me, my mind was very active. This was demonstrated by the marks in class..

There was a book which I had had for many years called *Chicks Own* and on one page there was a story of pixies having a town in the trees which was pictured as a town on sticks. My father thought how nice this would be to have as a garden ornament. He brought some scrap zinc home from work and made models of each house and joined them all together and fixed them on copper tubes. He made windows in them and fixed a lamp behind them. It was my job to paint it all with red roofs and yellow paint mixed with sand for the walls to give a rough surface. Working with my father like this made me aware of all sorts of metal work, soldering, and design. I have now passed this model onto my grandson.

Food was rationed so we kept chickens and my father made metal cages to keep them in. Many people kept hens in their back gardens, some in soaking wet runs that smelt badly, but my father studied the latest systems of keeping hens on wire floors, the bounce of which was supposed to keep them healthy. He made cages of his own design completely in metal. Rods were made from flat sheets of metal - mostly galvanised iron - bent into rods on a bending machine which I believe he bought from a scrap merchant and improved himself. He was always thinking of ways to improve or redesign things but never marketed the designs. He built a chicken shed at the bottom of the garden and we kept about two dozen hens. They laid well and my mother sold the eggs to the neighbours. My father always believed in feeding the hens well and we grew lots of cabbage and root vegetables. I remember collecting bacon bones from the butcher which were then steam cooked to a high pressure until they were soft. This made an addition to the hens' hot mash feed of an evening. There were people who said that it was cruel to keep hens cooped up as we did but my father had studied the space a chicken required and there was no doubt that our hens sang to us whenever we went near them and they always had food and water in front of them. When one stopped laying it gave us a very good dinner which in wartime helped with the rations. I also learnt to pluck chickens as soon as they were killed and became very proficient. I got three old pence for every chicken that I plucked.

One day my mother saw an advertisement for a laboratory assistant at Rugby Public School.

I had applied for a couple of jobs in surveyors offices but they wanted money paid to them for articled pupils which my parents could not do. However this was advertised for the princely sum of £1 per week. I went to see the Bursar who took me along to the science building to meet the biology professor. After asking about my education and if I had a bicycle, he decided that I would do and I got the job. The Headmaster of my school did not want me to leave but a call from the Rugby school soon overcame the objections.

I left school and started my first job in September 1941. It was all very confusing for me because unlike going into a factory where you were given a job to do, we seemed to be sitting down waiting for something to happen. Fortunately there was another laboratory assistant aged twenty-one.

Our job was to see that, before the start of each class, all the books and apparatus were laid out for each pupil. Most biology classes had between fifteen to twenty boys who must be supplied with a book and any apparatus needed for that lesson. The biology professor would tell us the day before what was needed, such as one earth worm in a tray for each boy. It would be my job to find two dozen earth worms by 9 am laid out in dissecting trays on the benches. That was easy because I could dig the earth worms up the day before, but when I was asked for twenty four frogs or dragon flies, it was not so easy to find enough samples! These students were paying good money for their education and did not take kindly to not having their correct samples.

One day, the professor came into our little office and asked for some *Proneous Sporum* which is a fungus that grows on Shepherd's Purse. It looks like white paint on the stem of the weed, he explained. Well, I asked my colleague about it but he had never seen it and suggested that I had better get on my bike and go and look for it. The laboratory was on the outskirts of Rugby so I was soon out in the country. But could I find any Shepherd's Purse with what looked like white paint on the stems? Every piece I found had no white paint-like substance on it. Eventually I returned to the laboratory with specimens of the weed.

"Well Jarvis, where are my specimens?" he balled. I hesitantly showed him what I had. "Well, boy, you have the right plant but not the fungus. Go to a stream or pond as the fungus only grows in damp places." I wished that he had said that in the first place. Off I went again to some very damp fields that I knew of and sure enough there was my Shepherd's Purse with the *proneous Sporum* growing on it.

I had many adventures looking for strange things like that. One day I was cycling down hill, with my coat in the basket on the handle bars of my bike, when I hit a stone and my coat jolted out of the basket and caught in the front wheel of the bike. I went straight over the handlebars and landed head first on the road. I lay there for a few minutes not knowing where I was. Fortunately I was only grazed as I had landed on the grass verge, but it certainly shook me up.

When I got home after work my mother and father asked me what had happened. When I told them about my accident, my father immediately had the answer. He said that to replace my basket, he would make a frame and a case to fit in it which would be bolted on to the front of my bike just like the butcher's boy. He made this and everyone thought that I was an errand boy! However, the carrier did the trick and I had no more accidents.

In spite of my left side continually giving me pain and making difficulties in some things that I did, I got on remarkably well in my job. There was a reptile pit in the laboratory grounds. But there were no longer any reptiles in it. It was about 20 feet in diameter and was surrounded by a concrete wall The interior was soil and rocks and had been neglected and covered with weeds and I was asked to bring it back to its original state. So, whenever I was not required for any specific job, I spent my time weeding and digging this pit. No one seemed to mind how much I did.

After about 18 months in this job I heard that a new Technical College was being built near my old elementary school and two laboratory assistants would be required for the chemistry and science laboratories. They were also offering a day release each week for study. I applied and because I was the only applicant with experience, I got the prime job in the chemistry lab. It was a lovely new laboratory with benches and chemical racks, and sinks with running water fitted to them. The chemistry tutor was a Dr. Wignal who was very proud of his new classes and made me polish the benches and clean the sinks every couple of days. I had a wonderful time there and the lab. assistant from the science department was a very good friend of a similar age to myself. We had many adventures in the underground ducts throughout the college, exploring where each tunnel which contained heating pipes and electrical supplies, led throughout the building.

During this time I was able to study for my London Matriculation exams both at night school and during the day release. I took the Matriculation in English, French, Maths, Chemistry, Electricity and Magnetism. Of course I was able to get a lot of tuition from the teachers at the college while I was earning my living. I had to take the examinations in Birmingham which meant travelling by train each day during the exams.

Sports day was held at the college once a year and much work was required to prepare for the visitors. Seating forms had to be carried out to the sports field.. I was helping with this when I grazed my left hand on a brick wall whilst carrying one end of a bench. Whether it was the sight of blood or the extra pain in my left arm I do not know, but I collapsed on the field. I was unconscious for a time and the next thing I knew, I was being taken to the hospital in an ambulance. When I arrived the doctor was most concerned with the lack of use in my left arm. I explained that I was paralysed, and my arm was put in a metal splint. My father saw this and said he could make one and I wore this each night for months afterwards. It certainly gave my left arm the ability to relax during the night.

This was in 1942 and young men of my age were mostly in the armed forces so there was not much competition when applying for jobs.

I would have liked to have gone in for architecture or a post in an estate agents but whenever I applied for any vacancies like that, I was told that a premium would have to be paid before I could become articled for training. Much the same applied to accountants. My parents could not afford that so I continued my laboratory work. However, I had similar feelings to all the boys who wanted to be part of the war and do their duty; I thought that I ought to be working on the land. When my colleague in the science laboratory was called up, I made enquiries and my uncle George knew an ex-apprentice from the B.T.H. who had extensive fruit and poultry farms in Maidstone, Kent. Because of the war he was always looking for labour. It was arranged that my father and I should go down to Maidstone to see what it was like. I was used to travelling up and down to London because my paternal grandparents lived in Bexleyheath on the borders of Kent. I also had experience of poultry because my father kept chickens. The interview went well and Mr.White (the owner) arranged for me to board with one of the permanent workers. So, I started another part of my life away from home.

It is always a traumatic time when one first leaves home. While travelling down to Kent to start my job I had new boots on and as instructed by my father I had put loads of Dubbin (a preservative) on my boots. As I travelled my feet became hot and a white mildew grew on the toes of my boots and I became very selfconscious travelling on the underground from Euston to Charingcross. I thought everyone would be looking at me. Of course no one had time to look at me, let alone my boots when everyone was rushing to get on a train.. I travelled on to Maidstone where I was met and taken out to Hunton where the farm was situated.

I had been brought up by my mother to be polite and unselfish. But I soon learnt that, out in the real world, one has to grab what one can or there was nothing left. There was another boy staying at the digs and he was greedy. With rationing as it was he tried to grab all the food but I made sure that I got my share.

As it was late August when I arrived at the farm, the fruit picking was in full season. The fruit was paid for by the box load picked and each picker was given their own named tickets which were put in the top of boxes of fruit. The main crop at this time was apples and the Newton Wonders and Granny Smith apples were sent to the packing sheds for boxing and sending to the wholesalers. Mr White had converted some oast houses into cold stores in which desert apples like Coxes Orange Pippins were specially wrapped and packed into trays to be stored for the Christmas trade. When the fruit was all picked I was taken to an Oast House that was in operation for the roasting of hops. The smell of the roasting hops was heavenly, and of course it was lovely and warm up in the roasting lofts.

When the fruit picking was completed I was transferred to the poultry farm which had about 5,000 chickens, most of which were laying. Here most of the men had been called up and the farm had an older manager and five land girls, one of whom was his daughter. Of course being eighteen, I got on very well with the land girls and we had great sing-songs while cleaning out the poultry houses.

About half the hens were in battery cages, six birds to each cage, with a moving belt beneath the cages to take the droppings away and collect the eggs, and long troughs for food and water.. The rest of the chickens were kept in deep litter houses which held 59-70 birds each. These were cleared of hens every ten weeks and dug out. I learned to use a machine plucker which consisted of two revolving discs which caught the feathers as the chicken was held against the machine. There was plenty to do but the poultry farm was some four miles away from where I was lodging.

That cycle ride could be very cold in the frosty winter mornings. One morning I got to the farm very cold and when my circulation returned I fainted, waking up in the arms of one of the land army girls. Very nice, but she already had a boyfriend. My parents heard about my problem and decided that I should move nearer to home.

The last train journey from Kent was in the middle of an air raid and I remember getting on the train from Euston and it was standing room only as it was packed with so many troops travelling north. Although the journey normally only took two to two and a half hours, this time we were an hour late arriving at Rugby as we were held up just before Reading due to an air raid there. When I arrived at Rugby station my father was waiting on the platform with a Thermos flask of hot tea. I was very pleased to see him as I had all my belongings and my bike to get off the train. Most of the soldiers were racing to the refreshment kiosk as there was no catering on the train.

We were friendly with a plant nurseryman in Rugby as my father supplied him with poultry droppings. He was opening another nursery in Towcester about twenty five miles from Rugby and he wanted someone to look after it. I moved back home and was taken to Towcester in his van each Monday and he would come over each Friday to check everything and take me home. During the week I would packet seeds and look after the plants in the glass-houses. There was a private hotel next door to the nursery where I stayed during the week. Behind the hotel were stables in which mushrooms were being grown. Some evenings I would help to turn the straw and hose it down to start it heating before planting the mushroom spores. I would also help with the picking of the grown mushrooms. The nurseryman at this time proposed me for membership of the Royal Horticultural Society. But my parents were concerned that the job I was in had little prospects of advancement. I had my forces medical whilst in Towcester and the doctor took one look at my left arm and leg and pronounced me unfit for the services. I think I got a C or D grade.

Meanwhile my uncle, who was apprentice training officer at the B.T.H. suggested that an apprenticeship could be arranged for me in the offices, which were quite substantial. It would be a new departure from their normal apprenticeship; a syllabus was arranged and I started work on the 24th February 1944 in the Industrial Sales Accounting Department as a clerk. For the next three years I moved around different departments including costing. I obtained my indentures detailing all the departments that I had experienced. When I had finished my apprenticeship I continued working in the Domestic Appliance sales department. Whilst serving my time, I had joined the Operatic section of the Social club and took part in several Gilbert and Sullivan operatic productions. *Iolanthe* and *The Gondoliers* were two in which I sung in the chorus, usually in the back row so that my disability did not show. I also helped with the front of house seating and ticket sales. I was asked to join the Dramatic Society and produced a J.B.Priestley play called *The Roundabout*. Priestley made fun of the working classes and as Russia at the time (1944) was fighting the Germans on the Eastern front in Russia and Poland, a paragraph was printed in the program indicating that no slur was intended on the Soviet Union whose forces were playing such a gallant part in the fight for freedom at that period.

The domestic sales department work involved sales correspondence, and I learnt to use a dictaphone on which letters were dictated straight on to waxed cylinders and then collected each hour to be sent to a typing pool. When typed, the correspondence was returned for checking and then signed and posted. I became quite proficient at this and very much liked the job .

My friend Peter and I decided to earn extra money by making cake decorations by casting plaster models using plasticine moulds made by pressing the plasticine round china models. We then sold them from door to door. To do this legally meant that I had to get a Pedlars licence which I applied for and got. Number 49 on folio 279/144. I used to take a tray out at lunch time because most people were at home then. The models I had were a sleigh boy, a Father Christmas and a snowman. I also made gnomes and small garden ornaments. Most of this was done in my bedroom and Peter got several original models for me to use. But Peter met a very nice young lady called Pat and his interest in the project waned. They were soon talking about getting married and since his father had died, his mother welcomed the idea and said that they could share her house. He asked me if I would be Best Man at his wedding. I was thrilled to accept. They had a small wedding at the Baptist Church and a reception in the Church Hall. It all went off very well and I made a short speech and toast and fulfilled my job as Best Man.

Chapter Three

FIRST MARRIAGE

My mother and father began thinking of the future and my father's retirement. They were looking at different properties including small holdings and they found a very nice place of 10 acres with farm house and stable in Church Lawford, four miles from Rugby on the Coventry road. The house had at one time had been the village blacksmith. There was also a cottage which was currently let. My father sold our current house and we moved into the farm. It had two large fields one of which went down to the banks of the river Avon.

We both continued to work at the B.T.H. and went into work together in my father's Ford Eight car He was keen to keep cows to get a regular income from milk after retirement.

We met other farmers in the village. One in particular took my parents round his dairy layout. He suggested that if they were thinking of only a few cows they should concentrate on Jersey cows because the milk was at a higher price per gallon and the cream, at that time, was at a premium..

Dad considered getting six Jersey cows and, always the perfectionist, he had a special cow-shed built with stainless steel fittings. My mother learnt to milk the cows satisfactorily. Later he fitted a milking machine and my mother had to become adept at clearing the last drop of milk in the udders of the cows. Apparently, if this was not done properly, milk production from the cows would slowly reduce.

Opposite the farm was a row of cottages, one of which belonged to the farm. It was let to a young family and they were looking for a larger cottage. They found another cottage and moved out, but before we realised what was happening the tenants' son moved in. I was hoping to get possession of the cottage for myself together with the nursery next to it. We took legal advice and were advised that a new tenant could not legally move in without our permission. My uncle Harry, who was in business in London, advised that we use a London solicitor to get an eviction order. He suggested that we use his solicitor and the case went to the county court. I learnt a lot about county cases when the solicitor brought in a Q.C. to take the case and he quoted precedents for this sort of thing and we won an eviction order. Imagine my pleasure when I moved into my own cottage even although it was only 'one up and one down' with an annex kitchen and outside loo.

I had in the meanwhile rekindled a freindship with Mary, the daughter of past friends of my parents. On achieving my own house, I hoped very much that Mary would consider marriage. However, she took one look at my 'palace' and said, "I'm not moving into that dump," and that was the end of that beautiful relationship. I was fed up for a while, but the greenhouses, garden and the fact that I was still working in the clerical sales department at the B.T.H in Rugby, kept me busy.

My uncle Harry (mother's brother) from London came down to see the farm and stayed for a few days. He was marketing Gnome Pens and I had made plaster model gnomes, so I made a sample model with a pen holder behind it. My uncle was impressed and asked me to make some which at an agreed price made a good marketing idea. I fulfilled quite a few orders for him.

One day he mentioned that he had a young secretary who was having trouble at home and he asked my mother if this girl could have a short holiday at the farm. When she came to stay I was very impressed. Her name was Valerie and when she returned to London we kept corresponding. She lived at Orpington on the borders of Kent, as did my uncle Harry, so I was able to stay at my uncle's bungalow and see her. Our relationship grew and we decided to get married. There were some formalities to overcome as she was not eighteen and her parents were separated so we had to get consent from her father. Finally we arranged the wedding at the Bromley Registrar office. My uncle Ken (Dad's brother) from Bexleyheath agreed to be Best Man. We got married on 14th May 1949 and my Uncle Harry organised most of the reception at a hotel next door to the registry office in Bromley. The wedding ceremony started without my best man, who arrived half way through. He crept in while the registrar was speaking and there was much rattling of what sounded like crisp packets being opened. We learnt afterwards that my uncle's motorbike had broken down on the way and the paper rattling was a film being put in his camera. My Auntie apologised most profusely to the Registrar at the reception after the service. The marriage ceremony went ahead satisfactorily and members of the family signed the register.

The author married Valerie on 14th May 1949. The author's uncle, Harry Watkins, gave the bride away

We had a very good reception in the hotel which had lovely grounds in which we took some lovely photos. Valerie and I travelled up to London and stayed in the Charingcross Railway Station Hotel. We went to see the musical *Oklahoma* that night but were woken up early by the shunting of the trains. We travelled back to Rugby, where my mother and father had arranged another reception for us at the farm for all of my Rugby friends who could not travel to London. They had made the excuse that they couldn't leave the animals for their not coming to the wedding in Kent. It did mean the we got more wedding presents to help set up the cottage! Valerie was quite satisfied with my little cottage, at least for the time being.

My wife got a job at the B.T.H. and we all travelled into work in my father's car. Valerie however did not last there very long. There were complaints made to my father by the head of the women's department that Valerie was flirting with the men. As my father had by then become Safety Engineer for the company, he could not afford any scandal, so she stayed at home and helped in my greenhouses. Her mother had been a florist so she knew about flowers and pot plants which meant that we could grow cut flowers and pot plants in the greenhouses. There were some 7,000 white lady narcissi growing at the top of the nursery which flowered near Easter. These we cut and bunched on a frame and took them on the bus at weekends to sell on the bombed sites in Coventry.

My parents were not very happy with the way our cottage was being kept clean and tidy. There was always some complaint; the door step was not cleaned or the windows were dirty or the curtains had not been washed. My mother would complain to my father who would give me a telling off in the car going to work the next morning.

Val and I made friends with an older couple, Mr and Mrs Tunnage, in the village who were quite complimentary about our nursery. Mr Tunnage owned some ground on the Coventry road near a small town called Bingley where there had been a coal mine. The site was mainly woodland, but hidden in the woods were caravans and buses which young people from Coventry had converted into living quarters and he suggested that we could do the same. Valerie was always saying that I was too much under my father's thumb and so we started to save money to buy a caravan. I heard about a cost clerk job going at Armstrong Siddeley Motor Co. in Coventry. They had gone into production of the Whitworth Jet Engine, and were looking for experienced cost clerks for the Cost Plus government contract. It was a different system to their car costing and required a new section to be set up in their cost office. Because of my experience and my indentures I got the job and gave my notice to the B.T.H. I found that I could get to Coventry by bus from Church Lawford and Bingly so we purchased a 16 ft Woodly caravan. I had saved a little and sold the nursery and cottage back to my father for the sum I had paid him for it, but I did have to get legal advice to get him to pay up.

The caravan was a four berth with a kitchen in the middle and Calor gas supplied the lighting and cooking. We had it delivered to the cottage, loaded it up with our possessions and Mr Tonnage towed it over to the site. We were in between two other young couples and there were plenty of willing hands to help push the caravan to the site and level it up. We were shown where the water tap was and there was a small wooden shed on the site in which we could house the toilet and the spare gas cylinder. We paid a month's site rent in advance and we were once more independent. Houses were very difficult to get, especially after the Coventry blitz. The housing list was very long so the authorities turned a blind eye to the sites with temporary accommodation on the Brandon road. We could always get a lift when other couples were going into Coventry. The community spirit was wonderful at that time. If there was a problem, most people would suggest a way out or help you. Valerie got some part time work and we soon got used to caravan living.

I was very lucky at Armstrong Siddeley as the costing was all new and I was able to spend quite a while in the factory, timing jobs in order to set a fixed cost for each operation on the parts for the manufacture of the jet engines. Each successive engine design was given the name of a snake. The first ones that I worked on were called the Mamba and the Python. It helped that at the B.T.H. I had learnt to read technical drawings.

On a Thursday we had to pay out the wages to the workers and since the factory extended over several acres and included the Siddeley car division, we got to know most of the workers very well. Because the production lines could not be stopped, we had to find each man and give him his wages wherever he was on the production lines. The Siddeley cars were very beautiful, with leather upholstery and wooden panelling.

The Cost Clerks had to have insurance cover, which the firm paid, to compensate for any monies lost during pay-out. There was also a Solarium with a Masseur, an oldish lady who was very good. I was to attend during working hours and have wax bath treatment on my left arm and hand and also massage on my left side which helped me very much.

I was also able to find a new market for my cake decorations in the housing estates near the factory. Each lunch time I went out with my case and called from door to door. I continued at Armstrong Siddeley for two years while we managed to live in the caravan quite comfortably.

One day I heard about a vacancy at Bluemels, a company which made bicycle pumps and accessories. The big benefit with this company was that they were situated in the village of Brandon, and so they picked their staff up in the morning and took them home at night by private bus and, being a smaller firm the employment was much more personal. My wife, Valerie, was also able to get a job there. I learnt how to use a Burroughs accounting machine and operate the Bought and Sales ledgers. This was a branch of accounting of which I had no experience and the trial balance which was used to manually make up monthly accounts was a very interesting exercise. The final monthly accounts were done by a part-time worker, an elderly lady from whom I learnt a lot about practical accounting. She had been with the firm for a long time so I had some interesting insight of some of the earlier employees.

At about this time, my parents sold the farm to a local vet, an Irishman, who I had known when I lived in Church Lawford. He and his wife were in their mid-thirties and he trained and raced greyhounds.. We became quite friendly with them and he took us several times to the greyhound track in Coventry where he raced his greyhounds; it was very interesting when we knew one of the dogs racing. While visiting the farm again I saw an old lantern that my father had made as a wall light when he first moved to the farm. Obviously it had not been to their liking as it was laying in the outhouse so I asked if I could have it and was told, certainly!

My parents had moved to a bungalow in Rugby and after a while we visited them and they seemed to accept Valerie at face value. The caravan had proved to be a comfortable home and apart

Church Lawford.
A number of picturesque cul de sac
lanes lead off the main village street.
These cottages are in Smithy Lane.

from Warwickshire and Worcestershire
Life, November 1982

from having to piddle on the gas cylinder outside the van each morning to thaw it out when there was a frost, we enjoyed living there. There was the weekly chore of digging a hole in the surrounding woods to bury the contents of the Elsan toilet and keeping the gas mantles free and clean for the lighting. We soon got used to that and made sure that we had spare gas cylinders and fittings because one never knew when the gas would run out.

One of my friends from work had beautiful St Bernard dogs and they often visited us because they could exercise their dogs in the woods behind us. He also kept bees and persuaded me to do the same, so I got a hive and learnt about them. At that time the Government was promoting bee-keeping, so I got a new hive, a colony of bees and a sugar ration for winter feeding. The hive had a metal frame which separated the colony from the honey frames so that the queen bee remained in the lower part of the hive and laid her eggs in this part of the hive. This means that the upper part of the hive is devoted to honeycombs. When I was looking into the hive after puffing smoke over the bees I must, in my ignorance, have let the queen bee into the top frames which were made of larger drone segments in order to make larger honeycombs. After I had reassembled the hive, the result was that the queen bee went on laying eggs which all hatched as drone bees. This meant that the worker bees were overwhelmed by the massive number of drone bees and the hive became in tumult and the bees began stinging everything in sight, including us and passers-by. That was the end of my efforts at bee-keeping. I quickly got an expert who closed the hive down and took it away.

I did some weeding and digging for a friend who was head gardener at Brownsover Estate. He bought one of my greenhouses when I was at Church Lawford and we had kept in touch since. While digging I began to have a pain in my left side. When I went to the doctor, he said that it was indigestion, which I frequently suffered from. We had been invited to my parents bungalow for Christmas and on Christmas day I became very ill. In the afternoon the doctor was called and when he arrived, not very happy to have his Christmas afternoon disturbed, he examined me and as he pressed my side I went very green and passed out. I was rushed to the Hospital of St Cross, Rugby. My appendix had burst and peritonitus had set in. Once more it was touch and go whether I could be saved. The only doctor who could be found sober was a foreign doctor who operated and left a large scar on my left side with tubes sticking out to drain away the poisonous fluids which had got into my system when the appendix burst. I had Penicillin injections twice a day and regular dressings three times a day and once during the night. It was very difficult for Valerie to work and get a bus from the caravan to the hospital to visit me, so apart from my parents occasionally visiting me, I had very few visitors. I was in hospital for ten weeks while my scar healed and because I lived in a caravan, the doctor was loath to release me. The National Health Authorities arranged for me to be sent to a Convalescent Home in Weston-Super-Mare for two weeks. This was in March, and Weston was very quiet but I found the area very bracing and my health quickly improved.

This being the situation I thought that it would be sensible for us to move down to Weston-Super-Mare. We put the caravan up for sale on the site, with the agreement of the site owners. A couple who were working at Bluemels but were holding back their marriage awaiting somewhere to live, quickly came to see us. They bought the caravan as it had all the bits and pieces surrounding the van as an established site. Another work friend arranged to transport us to Weston-Super-Mare by car with our immediate luggage. Meanwhile I had applied to the local Weston newspaper for temporary accommodation and we moved into a bedsit when we got to Weston. We looked around for a flat and found a nice ground floor flat at Uphill which was at the far end of the Front, not far from the Convalescent Home I had stayed in previously.

Next I needed to look for a job, and I was prepared to take anything. I saw an advert for a job as gardener for a property on Bleadon Hill which was not far from the flat. I applied to the owner of a very nice bungalow at the top of the hill which had about an acre of ground, some of which was fenced off for a pet goat. The owner was Secretary to the Weston Golf Club and the lady of the house kept Dachshounds. She had about twelve and frequently showed them in Westcountry dog shows. I took the job which was mainly to keep the lawns cut and the paths and drive clean. You can imagine the amount of dog poo that needed to be picked up. There was a vegetable garden which I planted for house vegetables. There was a housekeeper who came in daily, mainly to clean up after the dogs who were not house trained, and it was a pity to see such a lovely bungalow being spoilt by this mess. At coffee time she would call me into the kitchen for a drink and complain about the "sausages on castors" that made such a mess. I got on very well with the owner. I think he was glad to have someone with some intelligence to talk to. I kept the lawns and the edges well cut and suggested that I grow gladioli for him to have as cut flowers for the golf club and he thought this a good idea and gave me money to buy the corms. Not far away there was a wartime barrage balloon site which had gone wild. After making numerous enquiries the owner of the ground was traced in Bristol and I arranged to rent the ground for a very small fee. Valerie having seen the pet goat where I worked, thought we could keep goats on the balloon site as there were Anderson shelters there which would house them. We made enquiries and bought some British Saanan white goats with tussles under their chins. We bought six, four milking goats and two in kid. We housed them in the air-raid shelters with plenty of hay and straw and started milking them. We got the necessary milk cans and the goats milk did me a lot of good, health wise.

We tethered them during the day and they loved the brambles and stinging nettles. We went right through the summer of 1952 and were very happy. The goats milk made lovely cheese and some we sold. There is no doubt that the goats milk suited me and I became a lot stronger. Meanwhile the pet goat at the bungalow had had a kid which they asked me to dispose of at birth. But I had to milk their goat for them. The people who lived in the houses on the hill used to come out of an evening to talk to us and the antics of the kids jumping on top of the shelters to do a tap dance on the iron shelters kept everyone amused. But the winter was not so good. It was very wet that year and we began to wonder if we had done the right thing. We saw an advert in the spring for a cowman with a cottage and field with the job. It was at East Brent on a farm run by three sisters and they had a manager who had been with them since he left school. There were about thirty-five milking cows, machine milked and one of the sisters would finish the cows off. Since I had some experience when my father had his farm at Church Lawford, I thought I could manage the milking.

The trouble was that it was a seven day a week job, but we did have a cottage with the job. We bought a house cow, a lovely Jersey, which we kept in the paddock beside our cottage and with cow-cake as extra feed we had a good milk yield and we were able to make our own butter, milk and cream. We had brought the goats with us but found that they did not settle in the paddock so we returned them to where we purchased them without too much of a loss and bought a butter churn and the cow with the proceeds. East Brent is very cut off from civilisation and Valerie began to feel very lonely. It was not so bad for me as I had people to talk to but she was by herself most of the time and I had very little time off. One day the bull got loose and I tried to lead it back to its house and got tossed for my efforts. The manager had to bring the bull in on his tractor. This rather put me off farming.

Valerie at Weston-Super-Mare,
1953

37

Valerie had a portable typewriter and we decided to write to engineering firms in Bristol to see if there were any cost accounting jobs available. We went through the phone book and I think we must have written to about twenty firms when we had a reply from Clix, a branch of Ediswan Electric who made electrical plugs. They were a member of the A.E.I. group the same as B.T.H. where I served my apprenticeship. My Indentures were useful when I went for an interview and luckily got the job. Later in the day I bought the *Bristol Evening Mail* and found a bedsitter in Redland. I gave notice at the farm, sold the cow and got a furniture remover to take our bits to auction.

We were on the move again. Unfortunately the bedsitter was on the wrong side of Bristol for Ediswan but I was able to get a train round Bristol almost to the factory and started in the Cost Office. At the suggestion of the Cost Accountant, I started studying for the Institute of Cost Accountants examinations. I got exemption from the entrance exam because of my Matriculation and took the first Intermediate exam. I took a correspondence course with the Glasgow School of Accountancy. After a year in the bedsit the landlady asked us to find somewhere else to live. I think she thought that Valerie might have a baby which the landlady would not have welcomed. We had thought of moving to a flat and we were lucky to see one advertised in Brislington which was on the Bath side of Bristol. I also saw a cost clerk's job advertised with a firm called Bristol Plant Hire on the Brislington Trading Estate. This was near enough for me to walk to work.

So we moved house and changed my job. This job was entirely different to what I had done before. There were three male clerks who had to keep track of all the plant (cement mixers, dumpers, rollers, etc) and bill the hours worked as hire charge, transport and any extra costs. Because I came in last and the other two chaps were betting men, they called me Jack after the race horse owner and trainer Jack Jarvis who was very popular at that time. It was only a small company run by the directors who did all the plant purchase and management, but the company grew quickly, getting J.C.B. contracts and other heavy equipment; there was a lot of building going on in the West Country at that time. We also acted as sales agents for heavy plant for the South West. Valerie was able to do part-time typing for the firm and we began saving for the deposit on a house. We were very comfortable with Mr and Mrs Holmes, whose house we stayed in, and we were able to help them with decorating and painting as Mr Holmes was over seventy, but we felt it was time we had our own home. We found a small two bedroomed end house with a garage in the higher part of Brislington which we could afford with a mortgage. The garage was let to the district nurse which gave us an additional income. At the plant hire company, one of the clerks left and a new man started, a retired banker who had bad arthritis in his hands; his fingers were all knobbly and he said he had a lot of pain. He was certainly miserable and the camaraderie which we had had was lost. Although I had only been with the company for a year and a half I wanted to get back to costing.

I saw an advert one day in the *Bristol Evening News* for a position in the cost office of the Douglas Scooter Co. The company was situated between Hanam and Fishponds. I applied and got the job, but to get to the factory I had to get a bus from Brislington to the Tramway Centre in the centre of Bristol and then another bus to Hanam and then walk to the factory which was another half mile. I did this for a while until I discovered a ferry at Bees Tea Gardens which was not far from our house. I realised that I could go down to the Tea Gardens, take the ferry across the river and walk up the other side of the valley and be in Hanam near the factory quicker than taking the buses. I tried it one Saturday; down the 'hundred steps', across the ferry, up Cherry lane to Hanam post office and over to the factory. This was much better and cheaper so I arranged with Percy, the ferry owner, to cross on the ferry twice a day. If the ferry was not possible because of tides or any other reason, there was a footbridge further down the river by St Anne's Board Mills which I could use. It added another ten minutes to the journey. This became my regular daily exercise. I became known as the man with the umbrella as I always used an umbrella as a walking stick.

Valerie and I became very friendly with the ferry people and their family; grandchildren of Percy. He made swings and a helter-skelter for the children and got some skiffs and row boats for hire. We suggested one day that a tea cabin which was alongside the swings could be run at weekends as Percy and his wife had got too old to do teas any more as well as the ferry. We made one side of the cabin so it would open as a flap counter and Val and I ran the teashop at weekends and holidays. We stocked sweets and chocolates, made tea on a gas ring and sold rock cakes which I would have been busy making on a Friday night. I used Mrs Beaton's recipe. Because of the hundred steps approach it was mainly young people who came down, but it became quite popular. One or two houseboats were moored along the river bank. The river was tidal so any moorings had to be off the bank on mooring poles that would allow the boats to rise and fall with the tide. There was also a large concrete barge on which the boats for hire were kept. In one of the houseboats lived a rough character called Joe who worked at the saw mills and helped with the ferry and the hire boats when he was there. We bought a small houseboat from Percy which we could use when trade was poor in the teahouse. We also saved up and bought a small car from one of the clerks on the bought ledger section at Douglas. But we found that it had a cracked chassis and made him take it back. I enjoyed working at the Scooter factory and helped to install a standard costing system on the Vespa scooter assembly line. Val took her driving test through the Bristol School of Motoring and we bought an Austin A35 van; there was no purchase tax on vans at that time. Val was able to drive and learn on it. I passed my test after taking it three times, but my licence was endorsed "to drive a car with controls suitable for a weak left hand". The A35 had a hand break on the right side and the Bristol Driving School were very helpful and coached me through the final test because the first examiner said he wanted danger money!

One weekend Val said she was going away with one of her girl friends for Saturday and Sunday on the train. But she did not come home when the train was due and it was several hours before she came in. When questioned about it she admitted that she had been away with Joe, the chap from the boathouse at Bees Tea Gardens. When I asked Percy, the ferryman, he said she was often aboard his boat. I got really cross and told her that if she wanted to act like that she could go and live with him and she did. I did not like it but most of my friends told me that I was better off without her. So

I went to see the Solicitor who had handled the purchase of the house. He passed me onto his partner who handled divorces and he advised me to go for a divorce citing the weekend away when they stayed in a hotel in Taunton as man and wife. He got a copy of the hotel register with their signatures on it, and if it could be proved that they stayed in the same room overnight, then adultery would be assumed. My case was heard in the Bristol Assizes undefended and the divorce was granted, but I had to wait for three months for the Decree Nisi. I had to pay Val half of my assets which meant half the mortgage already repaid since we had purchased the house in our joint names and a valuation of furniture and fittings. I lived on the bread line for months in order to save for the repayments, but I cleared my debts and at last could live a normal life.

I continued to use the ferry to walk to and from work and actually obtained a promotion to the position of Internal Auditor. Douglas Scooters was taken over by Westinghouse Brake and Signal Co Ltd, and they required careful systems audits. I had become a member of the Amercan Institute of Internal Auditors and built up a very useful section. We were given a program of audit by the takeover company, which involved checking on all departments and visits to some of the customers who had Vespa Scooters on sale or return. Because Valerie had got a job as secretary to the Vespa Spares manager we saw each other occasionally. One or two people tried to get us back together but we tried one evening together and shortly after she rang me up to say she was expecting a baby. She knew that I wanted a family because we had been to a clinic for tests and had been told that there was a possibility of having a child, but although we had been married for eight years, no child had arrived, and I did not think that it was likely. I realised that it was certainly not my child so I told her that there was no possibility of us getting together and later I heard that she was blaming someone else for the baby.

During my audits I was sent down to an Agent in Islington, North London; he was shifty from the moment I met him and I had great difficulty in reconciling his stock of Vespas. He said his mother was a moneylender in the Islington market and had lost money which he tried to replace by selling our scooters. When I reported this back to Westinghouse we had to take legal action and got our money back but had to close his garage. The audit proved very valuable and as a result of that experience I carried out quite a few checks throughout the country which gave me experience in some very interesting investigations.

I kept the house going very well and let a room out to a man from Truro who was working in the Bristol Telephone Exchange. He was with me for several months until his training was complete. Then another young man came who was on temporary loan to a Bristol company. He became permanently employed and met a nice girl and they eventually got married and got their own house.

I continued with my correspondence course with the Glasgow School of Accountancy and passed my Intermediate exams for Costing and then took my Final. The first time I did not pass all the exams. Unfortunately the whole examination had to be taken each time, but could be done in two parts. The second part, the costing, had changed quite a bit over the time studied and more emphasis was made of budgeting and specialised costing and the Institute changed their name from Works Accounting to Management Accounting. This suited me very well and I was able to pass the examination.

The tea kiosk at the ferry was a great attraction during the summer months and I carried on making rock cakes. We had our regular visitors, such as two teenage girls who always bought Maltesers, and an elderly man who came regularly to hire a skiff and had tea and rock cakes when he returned from rowing. There was also a man with a shock of brown hair and a beard to match who rented a hut from the ferryman and worked on dredgers in the Bristol docks. I bought a canoe called *Tippercanoe*, a two seater, and enjoyed a trip on the river when I was not busy.

One of my friends from work was interested in canoeing and used to come down to Bees and go out with me on the river Avon of an evening. There was some lovely wildlife there and we used to pull into the bank and sit in the canoe and watch the kingfishers and gulls and lots of other birds swoop down to the water in the dusk and catch their suppers. He suggested one day that we should paddle up the Avon to Bath, possibly taking a tent to stay overnight on the way. So we set out one weekend with a small tent and paddled up to a low bank where we could land, pitch our tent in a field and camp overnight. We were lucky in having a fine night and we set off early in the morning to surmount the weirs in Bath and paddle through the city, having a very different view from that normally seen. We had breakfast in Bath and went up river as far as Bathamton when we turned round and retraced our journey. It was much easier going down stream with the current. When we got as far as Keynsham we had the additional advantage of the tidal flow and we arrived back at Bees feeling very happy after a good weekend.

Chapter Four

SECOND MARRIAGE

One day two nurses came down to the ferry looking for somewhere to stay overnight. They had driven from Chichester and did not want to drive back the same day. Since at that time I did not have anyone staying with me, I offered a double bedroom and they came back with me after I had finished the tea shop. The driver was called Beryl but known as BJ, the J was for Jane, and she was about 40. Her friend was called Angela and was about 36. They were both good company but BJ was the talkative one. We got on very well and at the end of the Sunday when they left, they arranged to visit again when their duty rota meant that they were both off duty at the same time. They made several visits during the summer and I was invited to Chichester to stay with another married nurse living in Selsey Bill. Her husband worked at the Tangmere RAF Airport. They were very kind to me and mentioned to me that BJ was married. I had already been watching Angela, the quiet one, and we got friendly. We went to a Nurses' dance at the Chichester Hospital the night before her birthday and at midnight the band played Happy Birthday just as we were dancing the last waltz and she was presented with a large basket of fruit. She was very embarrassed but had her photo taken for me. I think that was the night that I fell in love with her.

I travelled down to Chichester several times to see Angela and she would come back as far as Southampton and see me off on the train for Bristol. I would sing the Gracy Field's song *Now Is The*

The author with Angela, 1960

Hour which went, "Now is the hour that we must say goodbye, soon I'll be sailing far across the sea; while I'm away, oh please remember me, when I return you will be waiting for me." We would then kiss and I would board the train and be on my way until the next time we met.

We could hardly get together, with her in Chichester and me in Bristol, so she agreed to move to Bristol and get a job in one of the Bristol hospitals. I arranged for her to stay with Mr and Mrs Holmes where I had stayed before I bought my house. There was a problem with us getting married because she was a Catholic and I was divorced. I started going to the Catholic Church in Knowle not far from where we lived. We became quite friendly with the local priest and I started taking instructions to become a Catholic. We were sent to the Bishop's secretary in Clifton who took up our case for marriage, and it transpired that if I had not been baptised, the Catholic church would consider my previous marriage as null and void and with the Pope's blessing, we could get married in church. So I wrote to all the churches around Woolwich and Abbeywood, the area where I had been born, and obtained certificates from the vicars and priests saying that I did not appear in their registers around my date of birth. By the time we had finished, we had quite an impressive list of church certificates. The priest from Rugby interviewed my parents who assured him that I had never been baptised as I was sent to Sunday school at the Baptist chapel in Rugby which does not believe anyone should be baptised until they are in their teens and can decide for themselves. Having prepared all this information I thought I was nearly able to get married, but the Bishop's secretary said that my application had to be sent to Rome to obtain the Pope's approval. This was expected to take 12 to 18 months. You can imagine my reaction!

However Angela moved into my house and as time went on we got to know Bristol well and continued to do the teas at the ferry. Angela got a job at Fishponds Mental Hospital as she was not only a State Registered nurse but also had certificates for Mental Nursing. She obtained a position as Nursing Sister at Fishponds Hospital in the women's Geriatrics ward. It was two bus journeys from where we lived but there was a very good service both at night and early morning as she often worked nights. She was able to have a restful sleep during the day, prepare the meal and I would walk her to the bus stop in the evening. We had a lovely dog called Potter and she would walk to the bus stop with us but would want to get on the bus with Angela so I had to keep her on the lead before the bus came.

Imagine our joy when in November 1960 a phone call came from the Bishop's Secretary to say that our petition had been granted and we could marry provided that I was baptised into the Catholic faith. A baptism service was quickly arranged with one of the Knowle church sides-men as my sponsor. I had completed my tuition course so a week after the Baptism we got married, following the ceremony with a reception at a nearby hotel. Mr Holmes, whom Angela had stayed with, gave her away and Percy the ferryman was my best man. I was pleased that my Mother and Father came to the wedding. We went off to Bournemouth for our honeymoon; we had to take the dog with us and unfortunately she came into season while we were away and we were asked to leave the hotel because there were other dogs being attracted. So we came home early but had more time to sort the house out and get used to married life.

One day when we were shopping in Bristol's Old Market area, we had been buying wool for rug making, we saw in a pawnbrokers window, a ring made up of two snakes, gold with a diamond in each snake's head. I had once read a story of a sailor who had a ring exactly like the one in the window. We went into the shop and asked to see the ring. It was in fact two rings welded together and I could see that they were real diamonds because they

Following his baptism into the Catholic faith, the author married Angela in Bristol, 1960.

scratched the counter as I handled them. When we asked the old pawnbroker how much the ring was, he said that we could have the ring for the amount outstanding on the pawn: £3. We could not believe our luck and Angela bought it for me straight away. I still have it some 45 years later and I have cut many panes of glass with the diamonds.

Shortly after, I changed my job, having worked at the scooter factory for some five years, and took a position in the cost office at Robinson Waxed Paper Co. at Fishponds. We had bought an Austin van and I was learning to drive for the second time. The senior clerk in the office lived near to us and we drove together to work. This gave me a lot of practice in traffic. I did not say anything to the other people at work about our recent wedding because I had not been there long, but I had the ring which Angela had bought for me and it had been blessed together with Angela's wedding ring. The girls in the office noticed my ring and asked where it had come from, so I had to admit that we had just got married. This created quite a conversation piece for a day or two.

We settled down in the house and my neighbours welcomed Angela. One neighbour, who looked after the dog when we were out, had a daughter of 16 who often took the dog up to her bedroom and sometimes sprayed her with perfume. When Topsy, which was the name they had given her, came back we would know that Diana had been petting the dog.

As time went on we looked at caravans for our holidays and saw a very smart caravan called Carwide which was made especially for small cars, so we had a tow bar fitted to the van and bought the caravan and made a place in the back garden to site it.

My mother and father had not been very well and it was a long way to travel from Bristol to Rugby every time we had a phone call to say that one of them was ill, so we thought of moving up to the Midlands. We saw an advert in the national paper for a cost accountant and a financial accountant for Quinney's, a farm and dairy company who had their own bottling plant. I applied for the cost accounting position and went for an interview. I was asked how soon I could start. It was situated in the pretty village of Sambourne in Worcestershire, and I took the job providing that I could site my caravan on the farm until I found a house. This was

The author's parents,
Lily and Walter Jarvis, 1961

agreed and I gave notice to Robinsons and moved up to Sambourne at the end of the month. I think that Angela was getting a little tired of nursing and welcomed a change.

A recently qualified Chartered Accountant joined the company to handle the financial accounts and he lived in Studley, a village not far from Sambourne. There was a Catholic Church in Studley which we started to go to. One Sunday the priest asked us to stay behind after the service. Being a small church there were not many newcomers and after we had been several weeks, it was obvious that we were living in the area. He asked us where we were living and where I worked and we found that there was a small Catholic boarding school in Samborne called St. Joseph's which was being run by the priests. He told us that we could get Mass at the school any time we required it. We found this very convenient and soon became well known there. One day the head of the school asked Angela if she would like to become part-time matron for the school boarders as there were often minor ailments which really required a nurse. She accepted and would go into the school at about 11 am to see to any requirements during the lunch time. She became very popular with the boys.

One day I was walking toward the village from the farm when I saw a large triangular field with a pile of house bricks tipped in one corner. I asked around and was told that some bungalows were to be built there. I found out who the builder was and it was a private builder in a village nearby. I found that they were to be good quality and a reasonable price, and several were already

49

spoken for so I put my name down and paid a deposit quickly. I was able to walk round of an evening to watch progress. Meanwhile Angela had been able to sell our Bristol house for the asking price. We moved up to the new house and I was very glad to move out of the caravan. Angela liked the bungalow and got on very well with Mrs Quinney senior who was very interested in gardening. They both went up to the Chelsea Flower show on my first day tickets. I had been a member of the R.H.S. for many years since I had worked at the nursery and I had kept the membership going, often taking a day off to go to their fortnightly shows in Vincent Square.

I was able to develop my costing processes in the Quinney Company as there were several sections run by the three brothers. The eldest brother ran the farm and a milking herd. The next brother ran the bottling and orange juice cartoning plant and the third brother ran the marketing of the products. Quinney's had a large fleet of vans delivering milk, fruit juices and other goods and the vans would be loaded early each morning. They also branched out into plastic cartons in the form of Tetrapak with a pyramid container. The vans travelled within a radius of twenty miles from the farm. The management of this side of the business was quite an organisation.

What interested me was the idea of creating a machine rate per hour for bottling and cartoning and a cost per hour for the van distribution. There was a tie-up between Robinsons Wax Paper and the cartons used for the milk and orange juice cartons. I was able to use some of the experience gained at Robinsons for the new costing systems. I also became very interested in the farm costing which had not been developed. The Farmers' Union were advising farmers to employ farm secretaries who could submit statistics for national use. The local agricultural college asked if I could teach costing at a new secretarial course which they were starting and as Mrs Quinney was a governor of the college she volunteered me for the job and I wrote up a list of notes for them and took the classes for the first year of the course.

For a couple of years Angela and I had tests regarding starting a family, and since there was no sign of a pregnancy we discussed adoption. The Priest and Mrs Quinney, who was a magistrate, both said that they would help us with the application for adoption. There was a Catholic Adoption Society called Father Hudson's Homes not far away in Coleshill. We followed through all the adoption procedures, health workers came to see that we were fit people to adopt children and we had to go for several interviews before finally we were informed that there was a six month old baby boy available for adoption. The society had gone to great lengths to match the baby with our backgrounds and we realised why all the original questions which we had been asked were relevant.

We went to collect the baby in June and found that he had been born on the 21st January 1963. His mother was a girl of 16 from a town in the north of England. We had to agree that we would bring him up in the Catholic faith and that we would tell him that he was adopted when we felt that the time was right before the age of 12. There were all sorts of preparations to be made and our time was fully occupied with bringing up this small baby and getting all the equipment needed. We called him Sean, which is the Gaelic for John.

At work both the financial accountant and I found that after two years, once we had implemented the systems there was only very routine work left. So once more I looked around for a better job. A job for a cost accountant and office manager was advertised at a company called MPJ Ltd in Castle Bromwich. I applied for the job and was taken on to start as soon as I could. This meant driving each day about 29 miles and whilst it could be done, it was both expensive and tiring. I looked around for a house nearer to the job. We loved our bungalow in Sambourne but felt that if we were to continue with a good life, especially for Sean's schooling, we would have to move nearer to Birmingham.

Whilst driving through Castle Bromwich village one day I saw two new houses being built opposite the green. They looked rather nice and in a good position so I stopped on my way home one evening and looked round one of them. I noted the name of the sales agent and went home very excited. The next day I contacted the agent and found that there was one left for sale. Angela and I went back at the weekend to look over it with the agent and liked it very much. We put a deposit on the house and went back to

Sambourne to discus how we should sell the bungalow. We put an advert in the *Birmingham Evening News* and we received a phone call the following day and sold it for a higher price than expected.

We moved to Castle Bromwich and found that the house was very comfortable. The only trouble was that it was on the Chester road and the traffic rumbled past from five in the morning. Because I had been one of those travelling past, I had never stopped to appreciate the volume of traffic. However it is surprising what one can get used to and we soon ceased to notice it.

We visited Angela's uncle and aunt, Bob and Kitty McGee in Wales. They lived in a town called Maesteg near Bridgend. Bob worked as a paper slitter in the paper mills in Bridgend and in his spare time sold insurance. He was a happy sort of chap and we got on very well together. We went to the Catholic club on Saturday night and that was the only time that I ever saw Angela tipsy.

During the stay we visited a dog kennel, the owner of which was a friend of Kitty. We were looking for a pet dog to replace Topsy who had died a few months before. The kennels bred long haired collies like Lassie the film dog. The kennels had a bitch which kept failing to breed. We bought her on the understanding that if she did have pups the kennels would have them back. She was registered as Gold Dust, so we called her Dusty. She was very affectionate and Angela loved her. As Sean grew up he became very happy with her and she was very good with him. There was a school in Castle Bromwhich which held films for the children each Saturday morning and I took Sean to watch the films. I became quite friendly with the teacher who ran the show, sometimes helping him keep the children in order. One week the film was to be *The Adventures of Lassie* and the teacher asked me if I would bring Dusty to the film show as the 'sister of Lassie'. We duly went to the school and we went on to the stage after the film and Dusty sat down beside me while the teacher announced their very important visitor. Dusty did her bit and begged and wagged her tail and there was a huge roar from the children and every one wanted to stroke her. She was very good and seemed to be enjoying the attention until Sean rather spoilt it by shouting out, "that's my dog," however most of the children were making too much noise to hear him.

I settled down at my new job. MPJ was a friendly firm; the M stood for McNamara, who was the managing director and to whom I was directly responsible, the P stood for Powel who was an active director, and the J stood for Jones who had retired. It was rumoured that I had been taken on to become the new J in the company. The three men had all been tool makers and had joined together to make gauges. The company took over the agency for the manufacture of airguages from the Sheffield Air Guage Corporation of America. This American company was then taken over by Bendix Corporation which was a Blue Chip company in America.

I updated the accounting system so that the regular monthly returns could be sent to Bendix. One of my specialities in developing my training as a cost accountant was drawing up an organisation chart for each company that I had worked for. I had produced a chart for Robinson's Wax Paper Co, which their data proccessing department had found very useful when they had been formed shortly after I had left the company.

I produced an organisation chart for MPJ which proved very useful for Mr Macnamara as he expanded the company and when he met personnel from Bendix. My ability was recognised when Bendix took over another small tool company, Niemberding, in Germany. Dr Niemberding, who had started this company in a similar way to Mr Macnamara, came over to Birmingham to see how the English company had managed the take-over. He asked if I could spend two weeks in Germany to explain the American financial returns and the organisation required by Bendix. When Mr Macnamara received the request from Bendix saying how his organisation had met with their approval, he could hardly refuse my release for the two weeks. In due course, I was sent off to Frankfurt and met by a Mr Klein who was their accountant. We struck up an imediate friendship as we were both about the same age and family men. We found that we both played chess and were about the same standard. The company had a very good interpreter. The accountant lived in a small town called Denbach and whilst staying in Frankfurt I visited his home several times and met his family. He also had two children, a boy and a girl, a little older than mine. During my stay he also took me to the Black Forest and to a motor car museum. I got on very well with the company personnel and by the end of the two weeks we had produced a very good organisation chart and they had established several improvements in their financial department and designed the required returns for the parent company. I was rewarded at the end of my stay with a presentation of a travel clock with an inscription of their thanks. On my return journey at the Frankfurt airport I bought a model aircraft kit for Sean. Unfortunately I put the kit down while I was getting some refreshments and I turned round to find it had gone so when I got to London I had to quickly buy something else for him. After my visit, I carried on playing chess with Mr Klein over the company telex until someone asked what the coded messages were from Germany and we had to continue by post. Mr Klein brought his family over to visit the following year and we were able to return the hospitality.

Bendix were keen to expand the company so Mr McNamara started to look around for factories in development areas. These were areas of high unemployment which were being grant aided for new factories to enable industries in large cities to move to areas where they could expand outside the large cities. He looked at some factories in Anglesey but did not like the area so turned his attention to Devon. North Devon was in a bad way regarding unemployment because Dr Beeching was closing the railway stations at Bideford and Torrington. The Barnstaple to Torrington line no longer carried the clay exports from Petersmarland. The closure of the Bideford shipbuilding meant that the goods yard at Bideford was no longer viable. This meant that Bideford was doubly hit. The local council was also very helpful in as much that they were not only making ground available for factory space on the east side of the river but they were prepared to build council houses for key workers. After much consultation it was agreed that MPJ would buy a site on a hill on the east side of the river and that key worker houses would be built opposite the factory.

The first time I travelled from Birmingham to Bideford was by rail before the line closed. It was a complicated journey from Birmingham to Bristol, changing at Bristol for Exeter, then a change at Exeter with an hour's wait for a train to Barnstaple and change for a train to Torrington stopping at Bideford. I stayed at the Royal

Hotel which had its own door onto the platform. There was a hotel porter waiting for the train who looked after our luggage and showed us to our rooms.

The development in Bideford was much heralded by council officials as being a wonderful advancement for Bideford. An American owned company backing a factory for Bideford! However, many local people who had previously been employed in closed down firms, seemed reluctant to have new industry in their town. The factory was designed by a Birmingham Architect for a factory of 200,000 square yard space and was to be built in two stages of 100,000 square yards each. The first part was to include management offices, a warehouse and despatch bay. There were provisions for expansion of the manufacturing area to double the size when personnel were trained. The factory was built and the council, true to their word, built some very nice houses which they classed as 'executive houses' for rent by key workers. In order to prepare for manufacturing to start, we hired some old school premises in the Higher Gunstone area and installed some smaller machinery and started a training section so that we would have employees ready trained to start in the new factory when it was built.

Part of the area off Chester Road in Birmingham had quite a bit of house building going on and there was a lot of stealing of building material. One night someone broke into the back of our house and stole a small radio and a few books. Dusty was sleeping up stairs with us at the time and none of us heard a thing. After that we left Dusty downstairs in case of further break-in. We reported the theft to the police. They came and checked for finger prints but said there was little chance that we would get the stolen items back. The policemen thought it very funny that Dusty had not heard the thieves, especially since she barked the whole time they were at the house.

Nan, Angela's sister, who lived in Ireland, had one girl and five boys. The girl was called Alice and was the second eldest. She had helped bring up four of the boys and was working in the Kilmore Quay post office, but there was not much prospect of improvement. One day when we were on holiday, staying with Nan and Jim her husband, we suggested that maybe Alice would like to come back with us to Birmingham to stay and get a job there. She was very fond of baby Sean and wanted to look after him. She came back with us and when Mr Macnamara heard that she was looking for a job he asked me to bring her into the office as they were looking for a receptionist/telephone operator as the present one was leaving to have a baby. Alice was taken on straight away as he said he loved the soft Irish accent on the phone. His secretary made all the arrangements and she started work at MPJ and proved to be very popular with everyone. She was able to travel into work with me.

Dusty was very unsettled one Sunday and suddenly presented us with five puppies on the sofa. She was very thin after the delivery so we got the vet to give her some vitamin injections and one of the pups, a black and gold one was weak. We got him some injections too and christened him 'Black Jack'. We notified the kennels where we had bought Dusty, and when the puppies were six weeks old they came and took the four bitch puppies back.

We gave Alice an eighteenth birthday party and several friends from the factory came. The puppies were a great attraction and I think Alice really enjoyed herself. Shortly after this we heard that her father Jim was ill with cancer and she decided that she should return to Ireland to help her mother. I took her on the train to Fishguard where I handed her over in the care of one of the stewards on the ferry to be met at Rosslaire by Frank her elder brother.

Chapter Five

SETTLING IN BIDEFORD

I was often travelling to and from Birmingham to Bolton as MPJ were taking over a firm making soap presses which we were converting to applicators for crimping the wire terminals to wire harnesses for the electrical systems for cars. There was a lot of development coming over from America and I had to take the pay packets to the factory we had taken over until we could transfer the manufacture to Bideford. This entailed quite a lot of work arranging for personnel to be transferred and the leaving arrangements for those who did not want to move. I also had to travel to Bideford to interview some young school leavers to be taken on as apprentices. These young people had a short induction period in the Birmingham factory. Some of the boys stayed in my house in Chester Road while they were in Birmingham. When the factory in Bideford was finished we had some men who were prepared to move to Bideford as key workers. These and the trainees for the Gunstone school formed the nucleus of our manufacturing facility in Bideford. We advertised for a plant manager and we took on a man from G.E.C., but he was not very proficient and of course did not know a lot about our product.

Angela and I sold our house in Chester Road fairly quickly and were allocated a key worker's house in Goman Road, East-the-Water in Bideford, almost opposite the factory. I was very busy arranging the new factory move and trying to settle all the questions raised by the employees. The factory however prospered and manufacture commenced in spite of all the problems.

Mr Mcnamara retired as he felt that having started the company and brought it to this stage, it would be better to let someone else take over. Bendix owned another factory in Nottingham, the manager of which took over MPJ. He did not want a branch in Bideford and it was gradually run down.

I was in very good co-operation with the manger of the local labour exchange, having set up the factory and taken a lot of his unemployed people and when I told him what was happening he said he would keep a look out for me in case any suitable position should arise for me.

Meanwhile Angela and I had been looking round the area to find a house to buy. We found a cottage in a nearby village with a large garden which we bought and moved out to. It was in a group of cottages called Saltrens just outside the village of Monkleigh.

We had also received word from Dr Hudson's Homes that they had a baby girl christened Samantha Lucy Boyle born on 17th August 1966. We were anxious to have another child so that Sean would not be an only child as I had been. The adoption papers had to be processed through the Bideford Juvenile Courts and we named her Roseleen and finalised the completion of the documents on 31st March 1967.

Before we could move into Saltrens there were a lot of things to do in the cottage. It was over 100 years old and in the sitting room was a fire which looked like a urinal with awful tiles which did not suit the cottage at all, so I took it out and found a large alcove behind with a cloam bread oven at the side. We decided to open this up and make a walk-in fireplace. I got a beam to put up over the entrance to the fire and built a large log fireplace with the cloam oven lit with an electric light and a lantern over the beam and a copper canopy to take the smoke up the chimney. It looked very nice when it was finished. We settled into the cottage very well and we had very good neighbours. On the one side were a Mr and Mrs Gilbert and the other side was an old lady called Marjory who played the organ at Monkleigh Church. Mr.Gilbert was the head gardener at the Annery House Estate so I got on very well with him and took him to the Chelsea Flower Show one year.

There was a side entrance to the cottage which had been made for a horse and cart with a stable behind the cottage. But the driveway was not quite wide enough to take the car. I approached Mr. Gilbert to purchase three feet of his garden on the understanding that I would build a wall to prevent his garden bank from falling. His house was two feet higher than mine. This work took quite a long time because the soil had to be dug out and barrowed to the bottom of my garden, which was some two hundred feet long. I then built the wall as I progressed to prevent the soil from his garden from falling onto my drive. When this was finished I demolished the stable which gave a lot more walling stone. The site of the stable gave me room to build a prefabricated garage. We decided that it would be just as easy to go into Torrington from Saltrens as to go into Bideford for church and the garage owner where I purchased my petrol, who was also a Catholic, told us that the chapel at Torrington had only just been opened and required people to attend, so we went each Sunday. One of the men attending became very fond of Sean and offered to help me with the garage. We arranged for a delivery of Ready-Mix to be delivered for the drive and it poured with rain the whole morning. This was a good thing from one point of view because the cement did not set so quickly but we got soaked laying the cement for the drive and garage base.

There was a kindergarten in Torrington which Angela took Sean and Rose to as they were too young to start school. There was also a Convent in Bideford where we registered for them to start as soon as they became old enough.

Around this time Mr Gilbert died and his wife moved to her daughter's in Bideford. A new family bought the cottage and moved in. Their name was Fishleigh; the man's name was Graham and he was a carpenter .

In our cottage there was a problem upstairs. The bedroom floor sprung up and down as one walked across and I found that the downstairs parlour ceiling was not properly supported. With the help of my new neighbour we took down the partition wall and inserted an iron beam (RSJ) which rested upon stone pillars. This made the bedroom floors much safer and had the effect of opening the living room into two sections (dining and sitting rooms). Later the dining section was to be converted into the post office and shop. Whilst doing this work I discussed changing the small windows into bay windows with window seats to make the outside look like the famous "Quality Street". My neighbour who made the bay windows for me was so pleased with the result that he made them for his own house too.

It was not long after leaving MPJ that the manager of the labour exchange told me of a vacancy for an office manager at a glass factory which was to be built in Torrington by the Dartington Trust who were based in Dartington near Totness. The trust had sponsored many businesses in South Devon but none in North Devon. A Swedish glass company wanted to start a glass-blowing factory in England and Devon would be very suitable.

Torrington had high unemployment, was in the Government development area and had plenty of young men who were available for training. A Swedish man, Dr Wilhelmson (pronounced Vilhelmson), came over to plan the factory and start glass-blowing. When he arrived, he could not speak a word of English, but had a young man called Arne Linden to act as interpreter. There was an English speaking director, Colonel Palmer, who was local and called in occasionally. He ensured that everything was being organised properly. When I started with them I had to travel to Dolton, a village about eight miles the other side of Torrington where the company had rented a bungalow to act as a temporary office until the factory was finished.

The glass furnaces on the Continent are normally built on the ground floor and the glass-blowers have to climb up on to staging to dip their blowing tubes into the furnace and climb down again before they can start blowing. This wastes time and reduces the standard of glass. Dr Wilhelmson (or DR W as he was known) considered that if the furnaces were built in the basement and the glass-blowers worked at the level of the furnace mouth, this would save all the time climbing to the upper part of the furnace. These furnaces operate at about a thousand degrees centigrade and it takes three to four weeks, after lighting, to reach this temperature so the furnaces are only allowed to go out for maintenance, usually once a year when the factory workers are on holiday. I was privileged to witness the planning and building of the factory. The furnace room was the first part of the factory to be built and because the factory site was on a hill it was easier to build the basement at the lower part of the site, then the first floor and the bunkers for the special sand storage and the fuel tanks for the furnaces. After the glass is blown it must be cooled very slowly and this is done by passing the glass on a moving belt through a warm tunnel called a Lhear. This gradually reduces the temperature so that the glass is reduced to room temperature by the time it reaches the other end of the tunnel. This process is very critical as a sudden drop in temperature can result in cracks in the glass. Fortunately cracked glass can be used again by re-melting. When the furnaces were finished there was a great celebration for the initial lighting of the furnaces. The employees and their partners were all invited to a wine and cheese party in the basement of the factory. Angela and I went with Sean and Rose who was in a carry cot. Rose slept most of the time, but for Sean, as a four year old, the glass-blowing was a thrill.

One of the first things that I was asked to do after we had moved into the factory was to find some alder wood for making the moulds to blow the glass into. I scoured the woods around Monkleigh until I found some alder trees growing and got permission for them to be felled.

The workforce was to be started by importing twelve Swedish glass-blowers to form the nucleus to train local labour. A glass engraver from Stourbridge was persuaded to join us who formed the basis of a glass-polishing and engraving section.

I had great difficulty with the Swedish workers to explain our PAYE system of deducting tax weekly as they had been used to paying tax once a year. Mr Linden, our translator, had quite a problem explaining in Swedish what I had to say but he was very patient and got over details of the English system very well. Dartington Trust sent someone from Totnes every second week to back me up regarding legal and organisational things as Dr. Wilhelmson did not always think that I was right in what I was doing.

As the glassware was produced it was inspected and any product that had slight cracks or bubbles was put on one side. Dartington had an agreement with Portmarion Pottery to market the glass through their sales outlets. But the 'second' as the slightly imperfect glassware was called could be sold through the factory. To save any confusion, these were wrapped in newspaper and the top grade were wrapped in white tissue. The factory gave public tours during the lunch time and it was decided to offer the seconds glass for sale to the public at the end of their tours.

A very nice young Swedish lady (wife of a glassblower) conducted the public on the tours and I went round with her several times to learn the correct procedure and then, when she was not available, I too conducted the public, giving them all the information on the blowing of glass. My wife was persuaded to help during the middle of the day and we started the shop by a counter on a door supported by two tea chests which displayed our stock of seconds glassware. It has now grown into a lovely shop of almost 5,000 square feet, stocking other things besides the glass.

The work was very interesting and varied although the working out of the piecework rates and the payroll was routine, there was so much other work on the costing side that I had not encountered before. The problem I had was that most of the work was controlled by Dartington Trust and they had very strict ideas of what was wanted.

There was a glass-cutter from the Midlands who started with the company, training new men in the grinding and cutting of the glass and when Angela left he very kindly etched some sherry and wine glasses for us. I think his name was Fred Ralph.

I saw an advert for a cost accountant at the new American company AMP who had built a factory opposite the old MPJ factory. I went for an interview and although there were a lot of applicants, I got the job. I was sorry to leave the glass factory and Angela and I received lots of glassware as leaving presents. There was not much difference in travelling time from Monkleigh to Bideford as Monkleigh to Torrington.

AMP was a world-wide company and had a factory in Port Glasgow and I spent my first week on an introductory course in Port Glasgow under the tuition of the cost accountant there. As I was a Catholic and the men in that part of Scotland were mainly nonconformists, I took a lot of snide comments and teasing from them about my religion. But I survived and started at the Bideford factory having been thoroughly informed of the systems required and the regular returns to be made for the head office which was in

Stanmore, Middlesex. Because it was an American company the monthly returns and budgets were all standardised. There was not much room for any new systems or the use of any incentive, but with it being a new factory, there were always problems cropping up. I was asked to sit in on all executive meetings of the management group. The plant manager, a Mr Archie Pink was anti-Catholic and he was always calling me a 'Fienian' which is an Irish rebel, but we overcame our differences and I made quite a good position for myself, particularly since I was often called to head office where I reported to the chief accountant with whom I got on very well.

This was the third company that I had helped to form in the South West Development area and I knew how to claim machine and building grants and what questions the government inspectors would ask. I also got to know several of the government asset inspectors and knew that they were particular in wanting all claims to relate to plant numbered items. I was able to get the maintenance manager to show me all the claimed items and their identification labels. This enabled me to claim all the costs on grants including our installation costs. Although the Port Glasgow factory was in a development area they had had some bad experiences with the difficult Scottish inspectors.

Visiting the author's parents in Rugby, 1970.

Rose, Dad, Sean, Mum and Angela

The Monkleigh sub-post office closed down due to the retirement of the postmistress and the post office had difficulty in finding anyone to take the job on. I applied for the office to be opened in our cottage and when we knew that we were going to have a successful application we set about some alterations; the planning department said that I had to have off-road parking. We knocked down the front garden wall and built a lay-by in front of the house and my friend, the carpenter, once more helped to redesign the front room to accommodate a counter and a secure section for a sub-post office. Angela acted as postmistress and with my qualifications we had no trouble in persuading the postmaster general in Bideford that we were responsible people. Every Tuesday night we did our weekly returns and we bought an electric sign saying 'Monkleigh Post Office' which could be seen on the straight length of road so that there was no traffic danger for people pulling up at the post office. We also started stocking provisions for the local pensioners who could not get into Bideford easily. Our two children were both going to the Convent in Bideford and I took them into school in the morning on my way to work at AMP. Another girl's mother called Valerie took them home and I called for them after work.

As the post office developed we were asked to stock more provisions. There was a Cash and Carry wholesaler in Barnstaple which stayed open until 9.00 pm and we purchased the provisions each week according to requirements. If there were a few special things asked for we would purchase them in the Bideford supermarket and perhaps add a penny or two on to the price. We could still run a small profit overall to help with the overheads. Although AMP had a rule that an employee could not have other employment while working for the company, because Angela was technically running the post office and I was only handling the financial control, and because we were giving a service to the community, this rule was overlooked.

Angela was not very well during this period with stomach trouble. We did not pay too much attention to this, but as it got worse she persuaded her sister, Nan, to come over from Ireland for a few weeks to help her with the post office. Angela was suddenly taken into hospital with suspected bowel cancer and we went through a very worrying time while she was operated on. Sean had gone to St Boniface boarding school in Plymouth but Roseleen, who was only nine, did not understand what was going on and the Nuns at the Convent told me that they found her crying quite a bit in her lessons and she asked them all sorts of questions, the answers to some of which they could not give her. Many prayers were said for Angela both in the church and in the Convent. The operation was very successful and Angela came out of hospital after two weeks but could not do very much other than to rest.

Sean was very homesick at school and we tried to visit him every weekend. We were able to get lifts sometimes with other boys' parents and we ran a rota where each parent took turns to collect the boys for the weekend and return them Sunday evening. There were two other families with boys boarding from Bideford so it meant that if all went well we only had to drive to Plymouth once every three weeks. Sean took up music as he had already got a keyboard and a friend of mine who built electronic organs in Bideford had given him a few lessons. He was therefore able to continue in college with his interest and he took up the trumpet and joined the school orchestra.   St Boniface had a very good reputation for its music so we got him his own trumpet from another student, who had bought himself a new one, but could not get on with playing it. The first concert that we went to at the school, we sat right through the concert wondering when Sean was going to play and he had the final clang of the cymbals. But I must say that he came in at the right time with the finale!

Angela had made good progress with her health and Roseleen began to make much better progress with her own lessons. Next door but one lived a potter (Harry Juniper) who had bought the police house and used the office built on to it for displaying his wares. He had three children, two girls and one boy, and the girls were similar ages to our children but they went to the school in Monkleigh. They proved very helpful to Roseleen as they took her mind off her own problems. I bought a camper-van which was very useful for a changing room when we went down to the beach or the river in Torrington because all three girls loved to swim and paddle in the river.

I had some days holiday to come which AMP wanted me to take before the end of April when the new holiday qualification period started, and Angela and I had been discussing taking the children to London for a day to let them see the sights and broaden their knowledge. I asked them both what they thought; Sean did not want to bother but Rose jumped at the idea. We decided that if it was only Rose to go then I would take her on the night sleeper from Exeter and have the whole day to look round the city and return on the evening train called the Golden Hind. I was familiar with this journey as I did it every time I went up to head office at Stanmore. I got the tickets and reserved seats both ways.

When it came to the evening of departure Rose was very excited. We drove to Exeter, leaving about 7.30pm and parked at Exeter St David's Station and boarded the London train carriages for the night sleeper which was in a side platform and would be brought round to the main line to join the train at about midnight when the through train came in from Cornwall. This meant that one could board the train any time after 7.30pm and take the sleeping compartment without being disturbed when the journey started. Once the train started I found that the motion of the train sent me to sleep. The only time that I woke was at Bristol where there was a lengthy stop and a lot of noise on the platform. It was very exciting for Rose and I don't think that she slept too well but she seemed all right when we got off the train in Paddington the next morning. The train arrives at Paddington at about 4.00 am but there is no need to leave the train until 7.30 am when the steward for each carriage gives a knock on the compartment door to wake the occupants. We had breakfast in the station cafe before we got the underground train to the Strand and went up to the streets and made our way to Nelson's Column and Trafalgar Square. Then up the Strand and to Covent Garden and through to the Houses of Parliament. We went on to the Tower and joined a party to go round the Tower. After that we went for a trip on the river Thames and had our lunch on the boat. The Houses of Parliament looked quite different from the river and we passed Big Ben. In the afternoon we went to Buckingham Palace and Hyde Park and walked through to Charing Cross where we got the Underground to Paddington. We were very tired by then and since our seats were booked on the Golden Hind which left at 5.30 pm there was not a lot of time to spare. We were able to get a meal on the train which helped the journey to pass quickly and when we got to Exeter Rose fell asleep in the car while I drove home. When we arrived home after nine o'clock, Angela was pleased to see us but Rose was so tired that she went to bed after the smallest description of the day and a promise to explain in the morning. But she certainly enjoyed the day out and would not forget it for a long time.

Saltrens was a small community on its own. Although it was classed as part of Monkleigh and did not have its own pub, it had a very good cross section of vocational people. Besides us at the post office, there were the potter, Harry Juniper, his wife Barbara and their three children, Susan, Helen, and Nicholas who occupied the old police house. There was a garden nursery opposite which was run by a Mrs Stanbridge who lived in a very nice thatched cottage and sold a lot of her plants on a stall at the Pannier Market in Bideford. Further down the road were a Mr and Mrs Burridge who ran a small holding and made butter and cream and had a stall in the pannier market in Bideford on a Saturday. Across from them was Billy Whitlock who grew vegetables and whose transport was a Bubble car. Next door to him was Frank Tallin, who was a maintenance man for the South Western Electricity Board. Further on were Johnny and Dorothy Hearn. Johnny was the undertaker and made all his own coffins in a shed next to his bungalow. His wife Dorothy was a hairdresser and it was rumoured that he eyed up all her clients for the size of their coffins and made notes on them in case he had a coffin spare. His daughter, Fay, married a Dave Sloman who started a furniture removal business next door to the Hearns. Their daughters Tracy and Stephanie were of a similar age to Sean and Rose.

When Sean had any spare time, he helped some of the farmers. Mr Martin had a dairy farm further along the lane which ran by the side of our neighbours Mr and Mrs Gilbert, and Sean would often be missing and we would find that he had gone down to the farm to help with the cows.

Billy Gilbert was head gardener at the local estate and kept his own garden immaculate. There was a short road of council houses at the Bideford end of the village. One of the tenants, Ernie Curtis, ran an Agricultural Engineering business further down the village where he housed machinery for hire and contract. His son and several other local men helped to run the machinery.

There were several farmers in the area, some of whom had their papers delivered to the post office where they were collected during the day.

Next door to the post office on the Monkliegh side lived a charming old lady called Marjory Radcliff who was a retired teacher and who played the organ in Monkleigh Church. I filed her tax returns for her. She always had a cat, and each evening she would open her back door and call, "Kitty, Kitty, Kitty" and the cat would answer and come running back to her from wherever it had been.

Just outside the area on the Bideford side was a lovely old house owned by a Major Cooper and his daughter who was very fond of horse riding and kept her own horses in their stables. Nearer to Monkleigh was Pettycombe Manor which was owned by a Stanley Baker who dealt in second hand furniture.

It was a very interesting group of people. It could hardly be called a village, but nevertheless it had most things required for living a good life.

Sean with pet rabbit, 1977

Sean left school in the summer of 1979. He bought a second hand motorbike from someone in Southampton and soon became independently mobile. He had not quite decided what to do for full-time work and helped on local farms where he could. Meanwhile I had progressed in AMP and was on the executive committee and sometimes represented the company on the North Devon Manufacturing Association meetings; mainly because no one else at AMP wished to spend their evenings at meetings. I got to know some of the business people in Bideford and Barnstaple. One day one of the members was saying that he had great difficulty in getting papers and minutes to other companies, so I volunteered Sean as a courier with his motorbike. He helped where he could and, because he was polite and well spoken, he was asked about his future career. It so happened that the personnel officer at Hobarts in Barnstaple was looking for apprentices and asked Sean if he was interested. Hobarts was an international engineering firm making catering equipment. He seemed to like the idea and went for an interview, and started on a five year apprenticeship with a day release at North Devon College taking engineering drawing, mathematics and mechanical science, with workshop practice and general commercial studies. He did not do too well to start with but seemed to pick up as he got older and matured. He stayed with the firm to celebrate his 25 years with them so he can't have done too badly.

Sean's motorbike, 1980

Meanwhile Angela's health improved, but I could not help thinking that cancer never goes away. She did give up smoking after her operation but I think it was too late, the damage had been done. My office working times changed so I was no longer able to take Roseleen to school.

My father died and I went up to Rugby for a week, sold the bungalow and brought my mother back with me to live in a residential home in Torrington. A friend of mine very kindly hired a van and brought the bits of furniture and personal items from Rugby to the home. Mother did not want to stay in Rugby on her own as her sisters had died and she knew she would not see her grandchildren again if she stayed in the Midlands We got her a very nice room in the Castle Home in Torrington in which she could have her own chair and table linen and she settled in very well. Angela and I used to go to mass in the Catholic church in Torrington and there were one or two ladies from the church who visited my mother, which gave her a little company apart from us. Angela was able to buy a small Hillman car and because we knew when most pensioners came to the post office, the opening hours were quite flexible. We tried to visit Mother as much as possible and to take her out in a wheelchair when we could. She asked to become a Catholic and we had a very nice service in the home. Sean played his small keyboard and we sang some hymns and the priest carried out a very impressive service which pleased her very much. She would have converted earlier but my father was very much against the Catholic religion and would not entertain the thought. The priest was able to bring her communion regularly when he came to Torrington. The churches in Torrington and Hartland were served by the Bideford priest which meant that he had a very large area to cover. Since a large proportion of people in the area were in the older bracket there were many more call-outs for both the priests and doctors.

My mother died in 1981 on her 80th birthday She had complained about the heating in the Castle Home and I got a health inspector friend of mine to see the owners of the home with the result that she was asked to leave and we found a home in Bideford but I don't think she really settled. At the time I had to prepare the budgets for both factories and I was in Port Glasgow presenting their budget when my mother died and I had to fly back to Bideford for her funeral. The funeral took place from Torrington church and Sean was one of the pallbearers. The coffin was then taken to the Barnstaple Crematorium. I think my mother wanted to die as she was rapidly running short of money to pay for the home. The small amount of money she left helped to pay for the car we had bought.

AMP obtained a contract for the wiring of photocopiers with a national company and therefore opened factories in Exeter and Torrington and I handled the payroll of both of these factories from Bideford. It meant me travelling to both factories each week with the pay packets and travelling to Port Glasgow every quarter for budgets. Unfortunately the contract for the photocopying company did not progress as well as expected and we had to close the Exeter factory.

Chapter Six

MOVING TO IRELAND

A ngela's health did not appear to be too good so we had to close the post office. I heard that AMP was opening an office and warehouse in Dublin and the Stanmore office was looking for volunteers to work over there. I let it be known that I would be prepared to move to Ireland, particularly as I had a good deputy like Derrick who had joined AMP shortly after I started the cost office. He was very familiar with all the work and had very little chance of advancement while I remained in my present position. I was 56 and was keen on retiring to Kilmore Quay in due course, so if I could get the company to pay my moving expenses it would help. To my amazement, I was asked to take the job of office manager in the AMP office. We had a family conference with Angela, Sean and Rosaleen to see how they felt about moving to Ireland. Roseleen was just sixteen and about to leave school and she was very keen for the adventure as she thought Bideford was pretty dull. But Sean wanted to stay and finish his apprenticeship and our neighbour suggested that he could stay with them. They had a boy a little younger than Sean who would be company for him. Naturally Angela was thrilled about getting back home to Ireland, even if it was Dublin and not Wexford because it meant that we could eventually retire to Kilmore Quay.

We put the cottage in Saltrens up for sale and I went to work in Dublin on my birthday, January 29th 1982. The company paid for a month's stay in a hotel while I looked round for somewhere to stay. I eventually rented a house not far from the office in Tallagh. There was a sales clerk from head office who was called Ron Beumer whose mother was Dutch and father Indonesian. I got on with him very well and I always found him very polite and helpful. Eventually, we sold the cottage in Saltrens and I invested the money in the American bank that AMP used at a 19% interest rate. This helped to increase our capital while I rented a house in Dublin and Angela and Rose came over to join me. Ron was very helpful in our move and got on very well with Rose who re-christened herself Ross. I am afraid that she went from one job to another. Her strong English accent prevented her from getting some jobs because there was a built-in objection to employing 'Brits'. We did not expect this as I had not found it so with my own experience but I worked for an American company who was supplying parts for their manufacturers. The Irish were very charming to visitors who are spending money in Ireland, but if you came to take their jobs or settle in their country, it was quite a different story.

Ross did settle down very well once she found a decent job and when we were down in Kilmore Quay one weekend, she met a chap named Tom who was from Dublin but forgot to ask her for her Dublin address. He knew that we had a red British-registered car and that we lived in Tallagh. He toured the area, found the car, and eventually knocked on the front door to ask if Ross lived with us. Ross went out with him for eight years. He lived with his mother in Dublin but his uncle lived in Kilmore Quay where Angela's sister and family lived. Her boys were of similar ages to Ross and Tom, so there was quite an attraction for them all to get together at weekends. Ross was working as a waitress in a Dublin restaurant one day when the restaurant was raided by an armed gang just before closing time and the employees were all made to lie on the floor while the gang took the takings and the personal jewellery from the staff. This was rather traumatic and upset Ross for a while. Being young she got over it, but did not remain working there very much longer.

We were thinking of buying the house that we were renting and made arrangements with our solicitor to purchase, but when the searches were made, the title to the property was not correct. It appeared that the man from whom we were renting was not the legal owner. We therefore decided that it would be better to buy a house in Kilmore Quay where we eventually wanted to retire rather than settle for the next few years in Dublin and have to move again later, so we went down to Kilmore Quay each weekend and looked round for property. The money from the sale of our house in Devon had been mounting at the rate of 10% and had accumulated quite well, so when we were able to find a bungalow with an acre of ground with a good road frontage not far from Angela's sister, we made an offer and were able to buy it without a mortgage.

Angela was happy to be able to see her sister each weekend. Most of Nan's family had grown up and married and some had built houses in the lane adjacent to her cottage so there was room for us to stay overnight with Nan while we made alterations to the bungalow. I had the use of the AMP van and the company was glad that the van was not parked on company premises because there were gangs going round the industrial estates burning cars and vans which were left unattended, especially where companies were American or English owned.

AMP had originally agreed to pay legal fees for me to purchase a house in Dublin but would not pay for a purchase outside Dublin. This decision had quite an effect upon my future. I was aged 59 and considered another six years in Dublin with my wife in Kilmore Quay would not be very satisfactory, so I enquired about early retirement. The company pension scheme were prepared to sanction early retirement upon medical advice so I saw my doctor and found that he was prepared to give me a certificate suggesting that early retirement would be preferable due to a deterioration of my paralysis. The company considered this and consulted their insurance and pension funds and agreed to allow me to retire at sixty on a reduced pension. I agreed to this and spent the next few months updating the kitchen and bedroom with built-in furniture from MFI in Dublin while I had the van to take the kits down to Kilmore Quay at weekends. When I retired I was able to return for a few days to London where I was given a very nice leaving lunch and presentation of a case of Black and Decker tools. We settled down in Kilmore Quay to retirement. I had been with AMP for 27 years. I suppose that I had not done too badly considering that I was in a wheelchair at the age of eleven. I had only been unemployed for three weeks during my working life – that was when I was waiting for a job to start at the Glass factory.

The author's bungalow at Kilmore Quay, 1995

During my retirement I had plenty of time to talk to the fishermen and walk the dog on the nearby sand dunes. Angela would call to see her sister every afternoon but she began to have bad stomach pains again and we went to see the doctor and had some hospital appointments. I asked the doctor if it could be the cancer that had come back again and he said that after twenty years of good health he did not think so. But after much discussion it was agreed that Angela would go into hospital for a Barium X-Ray. The result was that there was cancer in her bowels but there was little they could do for her as the previous operation twenty years ago had removed a large part of her stomach and it would be fatal to do more. She was to maintain a strict diet and come every few months for a check up. She must have been in great pain but had morphine tablets to help. She rarely complained.

Meanwhile Ross had been unable to find a job and saw an advert for girls required as shop assistants in Jersey. We discussed the matter and I thought it would be better if Ross was away from home while Angela was so ill, so I took her over to Jersey and stayed with her while she applied and got a job with the largest department store in St Helier. The store helped her find somewhere to stay and she settled down very well.

Chapter Seven

IRISH LEGENDS

Kilmore Quay was full of history and some of the local people had a lot of legends and stories to tell. I copied some of these onto my computer in order to preserve them. We lived just below the site of Ballyteigue Castle which had originally been on the edge of the sea. The ground on which my bungalow was built and the burrow and surrounding land had all been reclaimed. The history of the castle was fascinating and is as follows:

Ballyteigue Castle, built originally on the banks of Ballyteigue Lough, and now situated within view of both roads entering Kilmore Quay, is adjacent to Ballyteigue Burrow. The drainage of the Lough was commenced in the 1840s to give relief work during the famine. In July 1847 the Board of Works suspended work on the reclamation scheme and three hundred men were thrown out of work. The project was, however, eventually completed and the land between the castle and the sea is now agricultural land and sand dunes. The old keep has always been well preserved and kept roofed by the occupants of the adjoining mansion.

The castle was originally built by Sir Walter De Whittey of the Norman settlers. The first Walter De Whythay (as it was then spelt) probably landed in 1171 with Henry II and a large force of 4,000; possibly the Devonshire contingent of Fitz Bernard, Sheriff of that county. It seems likely that he was initially granted land in the

Barony of Forth at Ballytra and Rathcastlemere, near Lady's Island Lough, but soon moved to Ballyteigue. The original castle was just a mound surrounded by a moat. Richard Whythay was one of the Jury at Waterford in 1266 and Henry Whythay was the first Juror on the Ostmen Temp in 1280. Sir Richard Whittey was summoned to Parliament as a Baron by Edward III, and his son, Richard, held three carucates of land in Ballyteigue in 1335 when it is believed that the first castle was built.

This castle was burnt down on the 12th June 1408 by Art McMurrough Kavanagh. It was a Tuesday morning following the feast of St Barnabas and he set fire to the castle and was paid a large ransom before departing.

Sir Richard Whittey was sheriff of Wexford in 1388. His son Richard succeeded to Balleyteigue and was appointed one of three gentlemen of the county of Wexford who was to provide 20 archers for its defence. A Richard Whittey died in May 1539. His son was 14 years old at his father's death and John Devereux became custodian. The estate then contained 3 manors, 3 carucate and 523 acres of land. Robert married Johanna, second daughter of Sir Nicholas Devereux of Ballymagir (the White Knight).

He died in December 1633. Margaret Whittey, his sister, married Michael Keating of Baldwinstown. Walter Whittey, son and heir of Richard, born 1603, married Eleanor, daughter of Hammond Stafford, of Ballyconnor. Richard Whittey, who erected the monument in the old Kilmore church (Grange) in 1647 - the only monument to be found belonging to an old Norman family - married, first, Catherline, daughter of Philip Devereux of Ballygir and after her death married Catherine daughter of Oliver Eustace of Ballynurney. Catherine, sister of Walter, married James Allison Bryan of Scar. Walter Whittey of Dungulph married Margaret, second daughter of Edward Hay of Tacumshane, widow of Pierce Fitzenry. Nicholas Whittey of Battlesown, one of the gentlemen of Bantry in 1608 married Margaret Cod. The Whitteys, according to some writers, constituted three different families, each having appropriate arms.

The Kavanaghs of Borris, representing the ancient Irish, were in the habit of making constant raids on the possessions etc of the

Normans of Forth and Bargy and feuds were of very frequent occurrence there on that account. Wexford was very often under the necessity of paying blackmail money to the Kavanaghs, who destroyed Ballyteigue Castle in 1408.

After the expulsion of the Whitteys, who lost their possessions in the Cromwellian Confiscations, the castle and lands of Ballyteigue were given to a Colonel Brett, some of whose descendants are still in the country. Brett died not long after occupying Ballyteigue and was succeeded by a gentleman named Sweeney, who married a Miss Shepherd whose father was an Englishman who came to Ireland in the reign of Queen Elizabeth. Mrs. Sweeney returned to England after her husband's death and was succeeded in the castle by the Colcloughs, a branch of the old and always popular family of Tintern Abbey. During the rising of insurgents in 1798 against injustice and atrocities by the English, poor John Colclough together with Cornelius Grogan of Johnstown, Bagal Harvey of Bargy and Captain Keogh, the Governor of Wexford were beheaded at Wexford.

John Colclough's only child, a daughter, married a Captain Young, and both lived in Ballyteigue castle until their deaths and are interred in St Patrick's cemetery in Wexford. The only daughter of Captain Young sold the castle to a Mr Edward Meadows and shortly after the death of his wife, (in the 1860s) the castle reverted to Mr Thomas Grant. The Grant family still occupy the manor and castle, which houses much local history.

Of the castle itself, the main tower and most of the bawn walls remain, also two smaller towers at the corners of the courtyard. The tower to the north-western corner contains a waterwheel, which was used to supply the water to the castle. The ground floor of the castle which has the usual vaulted roof was used as a dairy by the present owners. The walls of the main tower are about six feet thick and the stairs are in relatively good order. It is possible to climb to the top of the battlements and a deep hole can be seen in the passageway to the guard robe and this apparently was the entrance to a dungeon in the thickness of the walls. An archway over the entrance to the courtyard can still be seen with a machicolation above. Two or three steps remain inside the courtyard leading to the battlements on the walls.

It is said that Bagnal Harvey hid on the Saltees Islands before he was beheaded and was captured and held in the cellar of the Wooden House pub before being taken to Wexford to be beheaded.

The Whittey Monument at the Grange, Kilmore graveyard is the finest old monument now in the country and it was of the Whittey family at Ballyteigue. In the ruined church of Kilmore, erected in 1647 to the memory of Walter Whitty of Ballyteigue Castle, his wife, Helena, daughter of Hamond Staff of Ballyconnor, to Catherine, first wife of Richard Whitty, daughter of Phillip Devereux of Ballymagir, to Richard and his second wife, daughter of Oliver Eustace of Ballygurney. The Latin inscription is on the large slab resting on the base; over this are sculptured the arms, crest and motto. The arms of those of Whittey with the quartered arms of Devereux and Ennustace impaled on top. Of a smaller size are, impaled, the arms of Whittey and Stafford and the crest of a lion's head, affronted, which from its resemblance to a cat's face is said to have given rise to the story of "Sir Walter Whitty and the Cat". The translation of the inscription is as follows:

"As you are now, once was I:
As I am now, so will you be,
So, prepare for death, and follow me."

The legend of the Lord of Ballyteigue and the black cat; as written by Michael J. Whitty of Liverpool April 1872:

Every man, woman and child who lives between the Tower of Hook and the Fort of Rosslare can tell you all about the Lord of Ballyteigue, and his cat. But if you have no business beyond the mountain of Forth, I will tell you the story myself, just as I heard it from Dick Keating, an honest son of Crispin (patron of shoemakers) who though true to the last, served as a kind of speaking encyclopaedia for the good people of Baldwinstown. The country shoemaker is frequently a man of information, and it has often surprised me that the gentle craft has not produced more men of genus than Blomfield, Giffard and half a score of others.

You must know that all the Loughana (common people) about Kilmore are descendants of Strongbow's soldiers. The Keatings however, are thank God, of real Irish blood. Perhaps you may have seen their coat of arms. It is a fire and smoke and a hand and dagger, to show the sort of men all our family were. Well, one of Strongbow's Captains was a Whitty and a Norman as well. To him was given large tracts of land and he built the Castle of Ballyteigue, and ruled over all Kilmore. Twenty years after his landing he was killed defending his castle against the O'Kavanaghs, who ruled about Mount Leinster. His son however succeeded in beating back the Irish and for the great valour he displayed was Knighted, and called after Sir Walter Whitty.

He was a rollicking fine fellow, and spent all his time fowling and fishing, and a fine place he lived in for that purpose, to be sure.

The lord of Ballyteigue as Sir Walter was called was young and handsome, and you may be sure he wanted a wife, and why should he not since he had a fine castle to bring her to He looked about, and soon he fixed his eyes on the Lady Devereux, heiress of Ballymaghir who lived in the castle which is now the residence of Sir Edward Loftus. The Devereuxes were also Strongbonians and came from Normandy. Between the two castles ran the 'little sea' (Ballyteigue Loch) and Sir Walter, whenever he went to see his lady, had to cross this in a boat. Sometimes he had attendants and sometimes none.

One night he stayed later than usual with Lady Devereux, and by the time he started on his return and reached the waterside, a great storm had arisen. The waves were mountainous and the lightening was enough to blind one. Sir Walter, though brave enough was frightened, and what was worse, he could not find his boat. He bethought himself of turning back and spending the night in Ballymaghir. However it was easier said than done, for he had missed his way, and no wonder for the Slobs is a wild place.

At last, as luck would have it, he saw a light and making for it, found it was from a spyhole of a cabin. He knocked at the door, and a hoarse voice answered, asking, "Who's there?"

"The Lord of Ballyteigue," answered the Knight. "Let me in and I will reward you".

"Aye," said an old woman as she opened the door, "as your father rewarded me! The curse of the Murroughs rest upon you."

"Hush mother," said a young girl as beautiful as an angel. "Sure Sir Walter is my lady's lover."

"Lover!" bawled the old hag. "He shall never wed the Lady of Ballymaghir, Oonagh Murrough has said it."

"Why my good woman?" said the Knight, "how have I offended you?"

"Offended!" said she with a laugh, "Offended! Have not the Whittys ruined me and mine? Have they not murdered my husband, father and kindred? Have they not banished us from the house of our fathers? But Oonagh Murrough will be revenged! She has told her Ave Marias backwards, she will be revenged," and with this she fell into a fit, still screaming: "The storm! The storm! Who raised the storm?"

"A witch, by St Patrick!" exclaimed the Knight.

"Oh no Sir," said the girl. "My mother raves in this way whenever there is a storm. She is a little beside herself, take no notice, Sir, she is nothing bad," and she led the old woman away, and the Knight was calmed.

The storm continuing, Sir Walter sat down by the fire, and began to chat and flirt with the girl. She sang several songs in Irish for him, and when morning rose, she went out to show him the way to his boat on the strand. After some time he found his boat, and before getting into the boat, he gave the girl a kiss, and then she ran home to her mother.

When the Lord of Ballyteigue reached his castle, he could not help thinking of the old woman and her lovely daughter, and as he had not much to do that same evening he determined to pay them another visit. The old woman was out, but the girl was surprised and troubled at his presence. A kiss however set everything right and one kiss followed another, until finally he got the better of her, for as she said, poor thing, "a little thing done it!".

You may be sure that my gentleman didn't tell the Lady Devereux what had happened. And never a one knew anything about the matter until the girl's apron strings began to tell tales.

One night, as Sir Walter was returning from Ballymaghir, he found Oonagh's daughter sitting by the boat, waiting for him, sobbing and crying, as if her heart would break. When he asked her, she told him she could bear the thought of disgrace he had brought upon her no longer, and that unless he would promise to marry her, she would go at once and tell the Lady Devereux everything – the whole story.

The Knight was thunderstruck He well knew that if his lady heard of it, she would not marry him, and that would break his heart, for he was doting fond of her. He begged and prayed the girl to say nothing and that he would give her any amount of money. But nothing would do her but marriage. Then the Devil whispered in his ear, and he said to the girl, "well if it must be, be it so. Come into the boat and I'll carry you to Ballyteigue Castle."

In she got, but no sooner had he brought her to the middle of the Lough than he seized her and flung his young victim into the gloomy waters of the Lough. At that moment he heard a loud laugh, and presently a noise as if a thousand cats were fighting.

Terrified out of his senses, the Knight rowed for the shore, and hastened to his castle. But for the soul of him he could get neither peace nor ease, for a guilty conscience is a troublesome companion. Next day, lest he should be suspected of murder, he went to Oonagh's cottage, but found nothing there but an old ugly black cat. "Poor Puss," said he.

"Meheau," said she, and cocking her tail she followed him home, and took her place by the fire. From that day nothing was heard of the old woman or her daughter, but whenever Sir Walter went to catch rabbits in the Coney-Bawn (rabbit warren) he saw a white cat which met his eyes wherever he turned. His henchman told him that he often tried to kill her but he could not although she was destroying the rabbits.

In the meantime the Lord of Ballyteigue occupied himself, and sought to make his peace with God, in building Kilmore Church (the Grange). The match Between Sir Walter and the Lady Devereux proceeded. They were to be married, as it was on the morrow, and the bride sent the bridegroom as if it were today, to get some rabbits for the wedding dinner. He would not trust to any but himself, so out he went to the Burrow, but though he toiled all day there, ne'er a rabbit could he catch. Returning home at night quite disappointed he met the white cat perched on a bank of sand.

"Bad luck to you and all your tribe," he said taking up a stone and saying, "It's you and your like that have killed all my rabbits," and flinging the stone at her, he killed her.

When he reached home he found as usual the black cat sitting by the fire. "Moude killed Joude," (Cat I killed your kitten) he cried, but scarcely had she heard the sound of the word than she coiled up her back and sprung at him, and before any could save him, she had his throat cut. From that night to this day, the Lord of Ballyteigue is to be seen in the hall of the Castle with a black cat stuck to his throat!

The witch was burned at low water mark as she was found sitting in her cabin, after the bloody business was done by herself, and by nobody else as she later confessed. The white cat was her daughter whom she had also bewitched and it is supposed that she laid a spell on the Lady Devereux, for on news of Sir Walter's death, she drowned herself in a well in her garden.

Chapter Eight

THE LIGHTSHIP MUSEUM

A t the end of the First World War, a German submarine sunk a lightship off Arklow, midway up the east coast of the Irish Free State. Apparently the lightship captain had been warning all shipping that U-boats were operating in Irish waters and the submarine was unable to track its targets down. The captain of the U-boat surfaced near the lightship and told the lightship crew to abandon ship before the Germans sunk the lightship. The Captain of the submarine even knew the time of the next train from Arklow to Dublin. After the end of the war, however Germany was made to replace the lightship and a new ship was built at Leith in Scotland and paid for by Germany as reparations because Ireland had remained neutral all through the war.

The new lightship was built to the then latest design and was launched in 1918 and named *Guillemot*. She served for 50 years off Arklow until replaced by a lighted buoy in 1968. The lightship was then bought by the Wexford Historical Society and opened as a museum on Wexford Quay. In 1990 the museum was vandalised. Many of the volunteers in the Wexford society were retired people and the museum was not always manned and young people were having cider parties on board. Following this wanton damage, the society decided to put the lightship up for sale.

Some of the Kilmore Quay fishermen heard about this and were keen to have the lightship museum at the Quay. There had always been a lightship moored off the Saltees islands, near the entrance to the harbour, and many of the crew were from Kilmore Quay. A group of the fishermen called a village meeting and a committee was set up with headquarters in the Wooden House pub, with the landlord as chairman, and they decided to purchase the lightship and tow it round to the Quay. Cash was raised as a deposit and a helpful bank manager advanced the purchase price. The museum was bought and one of the fishermen who had a good sized trawler undertook to tow the lightship round to the Quay harbour.

This proved to be more difficult than was expected. One of the larger trawlers from Kilmore Quay went to Wexford and managed to get the *Guillemot* out of the harbour, but the lightship became grounded on the sand banks in the mouth of the river. Although at high tide the trawler floated clear they could not move the lightship and they had to leave it there for two weeks until the high spring tides when two trawlers went back to pull it free. Fortunately most of the models and artefacts had been taken off the boat and stored in Johnston Castle which was also open to the public as a museum. By the next high spring tide, two of the Kilmore Quay trawlers managed to tow the ship round to our harbour, but again they had to wait for a high tide to get the lightship over the bar at the mouth of the harbour. Eventually they were able to bring the ship to about ten feet away from the harbour wall. They arranged a boarding plank which could be lowered to the quay by a winch. To get on board one had to get a ladder from the quay up to the plank, walk up the plank and get on board to work the winch to lower the boarding plank. It was quite a physical performance, particularly because the winch was hand operated. I was invited to one of the meetings and asked if I could help with repairing the models and laying out the artefacts and I did rebuild some of the models.

I had built a sun-room on the front of the bungalow for Angela to sit and relax in the sun when she was not feeling too well. The doctor warned me that Angela was seriously ill and I phoned and asked Ross's employers if she could get some leave to be with her mother and she got a flight home and Tom, her boyfriend, met her at Dublin airport and brought her down to Kilmore Quay. She popped in to see Angela and then went straight out to a disco and didn't get in until the early hours of next morning. I discovered later that Ross had found it hard to comprehend how serious the situation was.

The following morning Angela had an appointment at the hospital for another X-ray. I drove her and Ross into Wexford and Ross went to the labour exchange and Angela and I went to the hospital. We had to wait quite a while and Angela did not feel too well. After the X-ray she was sent up to the women's ward. When I had her comfortable I went back to Kilmore Quay to get her night dress and the evening paper which we ordered each night from the local post office. When I returned, I brought her sister Nan and Ross back with me. I was surprised to find that a priest had been to see her and had heard her confessions. Angela was surprised to see Nan as it was her bingo night. We were discussing Ross's chance of getting a job when Angela suddenly grabbed my hand and turned green. Nan rang the bell for the nurse and I whispered to Angela that I was there. But she was dead when the nurse came. Unfortunately, Sean was unable to come over to Ireland to see his mother whilst she was still alive.

We were taken to a waiting room and a nurse brought us a cup of sweet tea. Poor Ross could not believe that her mother was dead. I was very surprised how the ward sister had Angela's body laid out and several nurses formed a candlelit procession and accompanied the body to the morgue. One nurse confided that Angela had been a nurse and sister throughout her life and they considered her 'one of them' and therefore wanted to give her the very best treatment. I must say that I was very impressed and pleased.

All the arrangements were made to bury Angela in the family grave in Kilmore Quay next to Jim, Nan's husband. After the funeral, we had lunch at the Saltees Hotel as some of our friends from Dublin had come down for the funeral and no way could we allow them to return without a meal. Many of Angela's friends came to wish me the very best and some of her bingo friends told me how much she cared for me. I felt very proud of how people responded. She had always been known as Nan McGee's sister and I was known as 'Nan McGee's sister's man'! Most people in the village were shocked and both pubs closed the afternoon of the funeral as a mark of respect; the Wooden House and Kehoes Pub and Parlour, where Nan's daughter Alice worked. Sean and a friend came over from Devon and he was a pall bearer together with Frank, Bim, and Brian, Nan's sons.

I arranged for a headstone and stone flower vase to be made with her married name and her maiden name of Kennedy engraved as she would still be known by a lot of local people by her maiden name, also her nursing friends would have known her as 'Ken'.

As I began to look after myself, the lightship committee asked me if I would take over the organisation of the museum. I felt that if I could immerse myself in something big, I would not think about my loss so much. So I became curator of the museum. The priest also asked me if I would join the church management committee and because I was familiar with computers I was asked if I could help with the weekly newsletter. I thus became the centre for collecting all the news events and happenings. I was thankfully helped by an ex-bank manager who had retired to the village who was familiar with computer work, and together we printed a newsletter every week for the church. Because we needed about 250 copies the priest helped with finance of a new laser printer which was a lot faster than the printer that I already had.

The lightship had been set up by the harbour quay and my first job was to clear up the inside and sort out all the artefacts and pictures into historic features for display throughout the cabins. I also prepared a history of the service of the present lightship.

There was a large model of Nelson's ship the *Africa* which had been smashed up but, repaired, would make a centrepiece for the museum. It was brought up to my house and left in the sun-room. I gradually remade the model and re-rigged it with all the rigging that had been pulled about by the vandals. It took me three weeks continuous work to get this done and there had been several near accidents outside my bungalow with cars suddenly stopping to see this large model of a sailing ship in my sun-lounge, and other cars following not pulling up in time. Then came the time when it was to be moved back to the *Guillemot*. It proved to be too big to go downstairs into the cabin where we wanted to display it. I had to

Guillemot Lightship Museum, Kilmore Quay, 1998

Lightship from the Bow

Left: Entrance to the Museum

Below: The author in the entrance cabin

take some of the rigging off again and re-rig it when it was displayed. Some of the artefacts had been stored at Johnston Castle while the boat was being towed round to Kilmore Quay and these were retrieved and repaired where necessary. There were photos and articles appertaining to the Irish Navy which separated from the British Navy at the time of independence (1918) and these were all sorted and displayed on one wall of the Oil Room which when the lightship had been in service had held three very large oil tanks containing the paraffin oil for the light.

The display contained photos of the handing over of the ships from the Royal Navy and the new ships over the years and some personnel and historic events. I was told by some of our visitors from Cork and Cobh that there were some pictures of ships which had been talked about but never seen. We had a group of Naval Personnel from Cobh who congratulated us on the display.

The five foot model of the *Africa* was so good that we had a plate glass case built round it and it became the centrepiece of the cabin. Another display of models showed the history of ships from rafts to a modern cruise ship, following the development of ships century by century. This proved quite educational and we had several school parties visiting. We did a very good tour to include a look round the lifeboat station followed by lunch at the Silver Fox, a restaurant in the centre of the village. The businesses of the village co-operated very well and I was able to type the menus for the Silver Fox which gave a short history of the village on the back.

I was also in touch with the curator of the lightship at Milford Haven in Wales who had a system of machines in each cabin which gave a dictated history for the relative cabin in three languages, one of which was Welsh. He had obtained financial help with the purchase price through the Welsh Society but I knew that we would have to pay the full price. We were having to pay guides to take parties round the lightship, whereas if we had these machines in the major cabins to give explanations in each location we could dispense with guides altogether. We got in touch with the suppliers who were based at the Beaulieu Motor Museum. The manager came over to see the lightship and suggested that we could install a station in five main cabins giving a description of what each section was used for and how it fitted into the overall function of the of the lightship. It was decided to use three languages; English, French and German. We got the trawlermen to help with the narrative and then the local radio DJ recorded the English version. A student translated the German version and a local teacher recorded the French. These were all sent to the motor museum where they were transferred to a master control disk. This control system was installed in the small cabin which had originally been the toilet of the lightship. This enabled anyone to press the relative button in any cabin and hear the descriptive talk in the language they required. This saved us having guides around the ship and meant that most times, one person could look after the museum.

The first year that we opened we had young ladies dressed in sailor hats as guides but the excitement soon wore off and we had difficulty getting volunteers. The narrative speakers in each cabin served a very useful purpose and reduced the questions asked by visitors to the person on the door at the entrance. It was quite noisy when all five speakers were going at once. I continued making models and new displays and tried to have something new each year. It was surprising how many people came every year, especially people from Dublin on their annual visit to Kilmore Quay.

Handover of the dictation units on board the Guillemot Lightship Museum

I booked up for a cruise to the Caribbean and then broke my ankle taking the dog for a walk over the Burrows (sand dunes) and had to have an ambulance to get me to hospital. I was taken to Wexford hospital, X-rayed and found to have a compound fracture of the right ankle. Of course, with my left leg partially paralysed, I could not balance at all. The nurse kept saying, "stand on your good leg," and I had to indicate that I had no good leg. I was sent to the hospital specialising in bone setting and had a plate and two screws put in the ankle and a special plastic cover to bear my weight. They also used special reinforced plaster. Of course, I had to cancel my cruise and with a medical certificate I was able to get my money back. The dog walking had to be reduced and I had wonderful help from the local people, especially the local nurse who took me into the Wexford hospital for therapy and progress reports and eventually, the removal of the plaster. You find out who your friends are when you are disabled like that.

Nan's youngest son, Brian, was having mariage problems, so he was glad to come and stay with me for a few weeks. The owner of the Silver Fox Restaurant, who I had helped with his business after his premises burnt down, by printing computerised menus and histories of the village, sent up my lunches each day while I was immobile. It really was surprising how much help I received from all sorts of people who one would not expect. For instance, the lady who lived at Ballyteigue Castle sent down some homemade tarts and cakes one day. The committee who ran the *Guillemot* Lightship Museum were also very good. The owner of the Wooden House pub sent a snack onto the boat whenever I was working on the lightship. We had a group of businesses who passed customers on to each other. They were the florist, the antiques shop, the restaurant, the men from the lifeboat house and the lightship. It meant that visitors to the village had an entertaining day if they wished to look round the village.

There had been enquiries from developers to extend the Burrows for a holiday camp and a fun-park, so when the owner of the land indicated that he was thinking of selling, the priest suggested that the village bought the land so that it would remain undeveloped and an amenity for the local inhabitants. A village meeting agreed that every household should be asked to contribute at least £5 over a period of time. Some paid weekly, some made their contributions straight away. We also drew up plans for a community centre, which would replace the old village hall, as it was 50 years old and in need of repair. Many fund-raising events were run and the fishermen and boat owners were very generous. The village committee, which was very active, applied for a grant through the EEC and received a 50% grant towards the cost of building the centre.

The number of visitors to the lightship grew until we were getting about 7,000 visitors a year on board. I was lucky to have a couple of Irish Television programmes done over the years as the lightship museum was quite unique. One was a historic programme during which we were able to get some of the old lightship crew together in the Captain's Cabin which had its original furnishings still intact. This made it a very interesting programme with yarns from some of the original crew of their experiences when they served on the lightship in storms. They explained the use of some of the equipment. I learnt a lot about the maintenance of the lantern in all weathers. I found that there was a way up to the lantern through the stem of the lantern support.

The second program was a children's club with between 20 and 30 children being shown around the ship. The questions they asked were wonderful and kept me busy answering them. The television crew took miles of footage and as they explained to me, it would all be edited and the resultant programme was very impressive and gave the museum a lot of advertisement.

When I was on the *Guillemot* all day, I would have my lunch at the Silver Fox and if I had a party for the museum, they would send my lunch in return for advertising the restaurant. Many of the parties went to the lifeboat station either before or after a visit to the museum. If the party was too big we would split it and take half in each location and then change over when the visit was finished.

One December Sunday I was at mass. The rain was very heavy and a strong wind was blowing inshore. When mass was over and we came out of church someone cycled past and called out to me that, "all hell is let loose in the harbour and your lightship has broken loose from its moorings." I ran down to the harbour as quickly as I could and sure enough the water was over the road and all the boats were being washed against the harbour walls. The *Guillemot* was afloat in the middle of the harbour. Nearly every trawler was damaged and the lobster-boats were smashed against the harbour walls. There was a thirty-foot gap in the harbour wall where the sea had smashed the rocks down onto the boats that were sheltering behind the outside wall. The road down to the harbour was flooded and also the fish and chip shop at the entrance to the harbour road. Everything was in a terrible state because it was too dangerous to try to get to any of the boats. There had been a tidal-surge from out at sea and it had just hit our part of the coast.

The Irish Government declared it a National Disaster and indicated that there would be financial help set aside for the repairs of the harbour and the boats, but as usual with these sort of things, no finance was available immediately. When the tide went out our

Aerial photograph of the Lightship after the harbour was rebuilt

lightship was grounded in the middle of the harbour. Several suggestions were made as to what we could do to get the ship back to the harbour wall. We hired some air bags from someone in Wales and tried to float the ship when the tide came in, but there was not sufficient depth of water to move the ship. The weight of the iron ship was too heavy! We had a suggestion from the Rosslaire Harbour Engineers that we should close off the harbour entrance and flood the harbour by pumping water into it until the *Guillemot* floated. We got their engineers to do this and when the ship was floating, the lifeboat crew fixed up a haulage rope attached to their tractor and gradually hauled the ship to the side of the harbour. This gave us a permanent berth. The cost was quite considerable but after much negotiation with the insurers, they agreed to pay for the Rosslaire charges and the lifeboat waived their charges because of the support we always gave them.

Chapter Nine

THIRD MARRIAGE

My life was very busy at this period and time went quickly but I did manage to book up another cruise to the Canary Isles. I was, however, restricted because I could not walk very well after breaking my ankle the previous year. This time I made the cruise and had a marvellous time. During the cruise I went on several coach trips when the ship was in port.

One day I was sitting on the coach for a trip round Las Palmas on Grand Canaria when an American gentleman said, "Damm it Alma, there are no double seats left again".

I was sitting in a double seat and opposite was a lady also occupying a double seat. So I called across, saying, "Excuse me madam, would you mind if I sat with you and gave these people the double seat?" The lady very kindly said I was welcome to sit with her. We started talking and it appeared that we had both lost our partners around the same time, both from cancer. I had taken on the museum to occupy my time and she had opened a second-hand book shop. When the coach stopped in the square of Las Palmas town, there was a museum nearby which had a display of old books and a maritime display; we both enjoyed the museum. After we had coffee in the square and then walked back to the cruise ship we arranged to meet later on board.

The lady, who was called Jean, was younger than me and suffered from ME. I explained that I had broken my ankle and was partially paralysed. The more we talked the more we found we had in common. We agreed to meet after the meal at the evening entertainment. It seemed that while I was living in Ireland, Jean was living in Scotland in a town called Kirkcudbright on the Solway Firth, in Dumfries and Galloway. At the end of the holiday we both agreed that we had had a very good cruise together and promised to get in touch when we had returned hom. We exchanged addresses and phone numbers and left Malaga on different planes.

I lost my passport and had to bluff my way home. I said that I had packed my passport in my suitcase. The only place where I was held up was on entry into Ireland where fortunately the Guarda on duty was from Kilmore Quay and knew me. I had to go through the process of getting a new passport and several weeks later my old passport was returned to me, cancelled. It had slipped down the back of the dressing table in my cabin and came to light when the ship was refurbished.

I had been very lucky throughout the cruise because when I left Rosslaire on the ferry from Ireland to Wales, I left a day early because of the bad weather forecast and I caught the last ferry to sail for three days. I picked up a taxi at Temple Mead, Bristol who recommended a nice hotel in Clifton for the overnight stay and the same taxi collected me the following morning to take me to Bristol Airport for the flight to Malaga to join the cruise ship. I had booked to share a cabin, but again I was lucky because no one turned up and I had a cabin to myself for the whole trip.

Needless to say when I got home I was very excited about meeting Jean and I had a very nice photograph of us both in evening dress taken one night by the cruise photographers which I was able to show everyone. I rang Jean the next week to see if she had got back home safely as she had returned on a Manchester flight and then had a coach journey back to Scotland. She had a good return trip without trouble and had reopened her bookshop.

My museum did not open during the winter but I was busy making new displays with new models for the coming season. One such display was 'The History Of Ships' with models from The Ark to current ships featuring rowing boats and rafts to galleons like the *Golden Hind* and *Victory*. There was a lot of work involved, mostly done at home.

I sent some flowers to Jean for St Valentines day and we arranged for me to go over to Scotland. I had an Irish Rail Pass which took me as far as the border, then I had to buy a ticket to Larne and a ferry ticket to Stranraer where Jean met me in her car. I stayed at her bungalow and we got to know each other and talked about our situation and whether it would be better for me to move to Scotland or Jean to move to Ireland as we felt that we would certainly like to live together. We agreed that she should come over to Kilmore Quay for a holiday and see which location would be best. We decided that it would be better for Jean to drive to Ayr, fly to Dublin and I would meet her at Dublin airport.

I had a very good friend who was the district nurse and ran the village antique shop. Her name was Bridget Ann and her husband, Dick, was a fisherman who I had helped erect a greenhouse in their beautiful garden half-a-mile further along the road from my bungalow. She, like a lot of other people in the village, was very keen to meet my new friend. I had shown them all the lovely photos we had taken on the cruise and they had all been impressed. When Bridget Ann had heard that Jean was coming over, she offered to drive me to the airport and bring us back. I was very grateful and when we met Jean off the plane we had lunch at the airport and they got on very well together.

When we got back to Kilmore Quay, I decided to fix up an evening meal at the Silver Fox so we drove down to the harbour and I called into the restaurant to book a table for the evening and was pounced upon by the waitresses asking where my lady friend was. When I said that she was waiting in the car, I was told to bring her in for tea on the house. So I got her to come in to the restaurant and they really made her welcome. We had a lovely cream tea and both the owner and his sister came to the table to welcome Jean. I was very proud.

I took Jean up to the McGees. Nan, (Angela's sister), had just had a new bungalow built and was very comfortable. McGee Row as it was now called, used to be called Dirty Lane as it was a sandy lane between the main village street and the New Road, but Dirty Lane had now been tarmacadamed and renamed Crossfanogue. The McGee family owned the ground on both sides so Nan's sons built their bungalows on this ground and that is why it was known as McGee Row. Nan had the original cottage, then Bim, the second son, built his own bungalow, then Nan had a bungalow built which was financed by Robin who was in Australia. Then a site was left for 'Cha', otherwise known as Brian, and then there was a large bungalow built by Frank the eldest boy and skipper of the fishing boat named the *Nicola Sharon* after his first two daughters. Finally Alice, Nan's daughter married to Paddy Kelly, built a small house, also on site.

By the time we had visited all who were home, Jean was tired but we had a lovely dinner at the Silver Fox and went home exhausted. Next day we wandered round the village and I took Jean on board the *Guillemot* museum. We had a marvellous time and decided that it would be easier for Jean to move to Kilmore Quay than for me to move to Scotland, provided that Jean could have a bookshop in the village. Having looked round the village we could not find a suitable premises, but there was an acre field by the side of my bungalow with road frontage and we discussed whether we could use this as a building site. The trouble was that it was very marshy. I asked a friend in the Wexford planning department about the field and was told that I would have to raise the level of the field by about four feet to bring it above the level of the road. There was already a draining gully under the road which took the water into the canal on the other side of the road and kept my bungalow dry.

The Ministry of the Marine had decided to put a project through to reduce the floor of the harbour by six to eight metres to allow the harbour to be non-tidal. It would make a big difference to the boats as they would no longer be dependant on tide times and could come and go at any time. It would also mean the there could be a marina and yacht anchorage and there would not be a sand-bank in the harbour mouth at low tide. There were several public meetings regarding the positioning of boats and of course there were arguments with regard to what should be done with the *Guillemot*. Eventually it was agreed the lightship should be positioned against the quay so that the public could board the ship directly from the quay instead of crossing the gang plank. This had put quite a few people off from coming aboard. It also meant that the *Guillemot* was aground most of the time and was not floating at high tide.

The work started on the harbour, which meant damming the entrance and pumping all the water out and taking all the rocks and sand out to a depth of some fifteen to twenty feet. When the water was let back into the harbour, there would be a depth of water at all times, although still rising up and down with the tide. There were many thirty-ton lorries to take the rocks and shale away to be dumped in in-fill areas some twenty miles up the coast. I became quite friendly with the engineers in charge of the harbour works who used to come aboard the *Guillemot* to watch their blasting effects. There would be a siren sound to warn us to take cover before a blast would take place, and the workers could look out of our portholes quite safely during explosions. Eventually our lightship was left on top of a sand castle, while all around the rock and sand had been excavated.

Whilst talking to one of the engineers, he complained of the cost of disposing of the excavations and I mentioned my marshy field which needed filling up to road level and he came to see the field and said that he would be delighted to divert some of the lorries, and not only would he dump the shale but would level and compound it. It took some 350 lorries each with 30 tons of excavated material to cover the whole field, and before it was levelled it looked like a lunar landscape, but after levelling and compressing it made a very good building site. The only trouble was that they had gone straight across the stream and blocked it up. After a few days I woke up to find the bungalow surrounded by water. The goldfish in my pond had swum away in the flood. I phoned the digger driver who was very sympathetic and got some concrete pipes about two feet in diameter and dug a trench through my new field to the viaduct under the road and installed the pipe across the site to take all the water away.

One day when Jean was visiting me, we sat down and designed a bungalow with a bookshop at one end and a large sitting room with a feature fireplace at the other with all the services and bedrooms in between. I drew it out properly and gave it to an architect friend to draw up to meet planning requirements. We sorted the power and sewage requirements out and hired an architectural supervisory service to oversee the building arrangements. The Irish local council were bringing in so many by-laws that it was better to hire professional people to ensure that the plans would be passed. It was decided to build the bungalow on a concrete ramp to prevent subsidence. When the bungalow was being built we found that there was a large roof space sufficient to build a flat, so we amended the contract and put a self-contained flat in the roof over the centre part of the building, together with two gable windows. It was a very nice building when it was finished, although its cost had risen much above the original estimate. However, we had a bungalow for ourselves, a shop for the books and a flat above with its own kitchen, bathroom, bedroom and large lounge. It made a very nice place for Ross and her partner, who were in Jersey at that time, or Sean and his new girlfriend from Devon, to come and stay and be quite independent if they wanted to. Jean, when she saw how committed I was to Kilmore Quay, agreed to sell her bungalow and let the bookshop, so I took some fifty factory cartons over in December 1995 and we packed up all her books and furniture. I returned to Ireland and brought a furniture van from Wexford and took the books and furniture over to be stored in Wexford until the new bungalow was finished. We were lucky to find some very nice bookcases to fit out the book-shop. We also found a carpet wholesaler who undertook to carpet the whole house including the bookshop.

We had moved about 6,000 second-hand books which we had to re-price in euros. It made a very impressive display and our priest came in to see what we were doing and then announced our open-ing from the pulpit at mass the following week! He gave us a very good recommendation and we were amazed the following week that a number of people came into the bookshop, saying that Father had said that they should come in. The priests in Ireland have a big influence on their congregation. We also let it be known that we would buy any second-hand books in good condition and had a lot of people bring their old books in. We did have one problem when some young people tried to sell books from the local school library, but we had a phone call from the head teacher and returned any of their books at a loss to us and soon found out who was involved.

Meanwhile, the *Guillemot* museum continued to expand and during the winter several more exhibits were completed.

Willowsand, the newly-built bungalow and bookshop at Kilmore Quay, 1997

The ground surrounding our new bungalow was shale from the bottom of the harbour, and people said that we would never get any plants to grow. This was a challenge and I was determined to show how wrong they were. I managed to buy bags of mushroom compost which I spread over the surface to a depth of 18 inches. Then we had a lorry load of top soil and finally a couple of loads of bark chippings which kept the soil damp. There was a very good Garden Centre in Rosslaire, about 14 miles away, who specialised in plants for the sea coast and we spent about £100 in stocking up with willows and hardy shrubs. I laid out the grounds with large rocks and shingle in beds with the borders surrounding them. The Wexford Planning Department insisted on a large off-the-road car park and instead of a square park, Jean laid out a circular area which we had tarmacadamed by the side of the shop. There was a local handyman called Paddy who was known to go on a binge every so often and so no one would employ him because he was unreliable, but I always got on very well with him and gave him the job and the materials and left him to get on with it. This seemed to suit him very well. He was also keen to discuss the over-all plan which Jean and I had laid out. I collected rocks from my own site and the site next door, where they had seen our deposits from the harbour and requested the same. The stones that were mixed in with the shale were ideal for a dry wall which I built right along the road front. Paddy put up fencing and some partitioning between the shop and the house, and the rest of my ground and the other side of the premises. At the end of my field was a right of way to the other ground behind. This gave me quite an advantage because unless I sold the right of way, no road could be put through for the building of houses behind me.

Some way behind us was Ballyteigh Castle and the sea had once gone right up to the moat of the castle. There had been a large reclamation project in the mid-19th century when unemployment was very bad in Southern Ireland and the potato famine had caused such terror. People were given plots of land to grow their own food, but much of this had never been registered in the Dublin land registry. When we first bought the original bungalow and ground and I still lived in Dublin, we assumed that the Dublin Solicitor who acted for us had carried out the searches correctly, but when Jean and I came to transfer some of the land from my name to hers we found that the ground was not registered properly. It was lucky that I knew most of the villagers and was able to trace who had originally owned the ground and get the land properly registered. It seemed that land was left to people in wills and they assumed that they had been given the land but never reregistered it. This meant that the registered land-owner was most likely dead. The solicitors had had a terrible time sorting it all out. But it had to be done and I was able to sell a building site beyond the new house and shop

We did some research in trying to find an Irish name for the house, and eventually decided on Willowsand. My old bungalow was rented out to an English couple who had come over on holiday and liked the area so much that they decided to stay.

After two years living together, Jean and I decided to get married. This was a financial as well as a domestic decision because Jean had a very good pension from her late husband's civil service employment but one of the clauses in the pension fund was

The author with Jean in Monaco, on a cruise

that if a widow remarried the pension stopped. It took me quite a while to persuade Jean to give up her pension, but as the bookshop turnover improved, she was happy to agree and we arranged to get married in November 1997.

In Ireland, one has to get married in the Registry Office and again in the church if both parties are not Catholic. If both parties are Catholic the Registrar will come to the church. The Registrar for the county of Wexford lived in Enniscorthy about 12 miles north of Wexford town, and he was the owner of a brewery. We went to see him and arranged for the banns to be published and November 17th, a Saturday, was set for our wedding.

I was a member of the Wexford Tourist Group because of my connection with the lightship museum and the group visited some of the major attractions. During one of these visits we had lunch at a hotel near Enniscorthy which had lovely four poster beds in their bridal suites with gold taps in the en-suites. So I arranged for us to stay for our wedding night at this hotel. Sean, my son, and his partner were our witnesses for the marriage ceremony which took place in the Registrar's house in the brewery. The house had a large reception area which the Registrar's wife had decorated with flowers and they made us very welcome. By the time the ceremony was over and all the forms had been signed, it was pouring with rain. We drove into the city and went for lunch. Sean and his partner then took the flowers back to my bungalow at Kilmore Quay and stayed the night. We went to the special hotel and had a very nice evening meal and retired to our four poster bed. The Priest at Kilmore Quay had written a special personal service for us as Jean was not a Catholic. Because I did so much for the church with the printing and publishing of the weekly newsletter, he certainly made it quite a ceremony and a good number of villagers were in the church to greet us.

After the service we all retired to Kehoes Pub and Parlour, opposite the church, and had another reception. Alice, Nan's daughter, who worked at Kehoes, made sure we were well looked after and most of Angela's family were there to wish us success. It was quite a weekend and Jean and I were glad to rest when it was over.

Meanwhile life continued very smoothly, after we moved into Willowsand and we started the bookshop which grew in leaps and bounds. We had many local people bringing books in for us to value and buy if they were good quality. Jean would often go off to buy complete collections of books from people who were moving house or had lost a relative. If I was not on duty on the *Guillemot*, I would stand in at the bookshop while Jean was out buying books. We also made two or three visits to Hay-on-Wye in South Wales to increase our stocks of books. Hay-on-Wye is a village which is devoted to second-hand book sales. There are many bookshops, some small and some very large. There is a cinema which has been completely turned into a large bookshop and a warehouse with several floors of diferent types of books. Needless to say, we always came back with a large selection of books to increase our stocks in the bookshop and Jean believed in 'small profit, quick return,' so she priced the books accordingly.

There was a period in Ireland when the electric supply was not very reliable and one Christmas we were very lucky. We were going to be having our Christmas lunch at home and had been asked to the McGees for the afternoon, so we decided to ask our friend Nicky at the Silver Fox if we could have a Christmas lunch sent up as a take-away on Christmas Eve. He was selling his Christmas special, so he put by two very nice lunches and we collected them before he closed. On Christmas morning there was a power cut with the result that no one was able to cook their lunch. All we had to do was to warm our meals up over a Calor Gas ring and we had a lovely lunch. The power came back on at midday but everyone spent most of their afternoons cooking their Christmas turkey. There was a lot of grumbling in the pubs that night.

After much hard work, the garden surounding Willowsand was taking shape. Our plants grew very well and we proved that a garden could be made so near to the coast provided that shelter could be given from the salt winds.

The author with daughter Rose at Pirates Cove, Ireland

Chapter Ten

RETURN TO ENGLAND

We decided that we would be better returning to England in the long term, but first I had to get someone to take over the *Guillemot* museum. This was not at all easy as none of the committee wished to take over and there was quite a bank overdraft to be cleared. I advertised for someone to purchase the museum and had the contents valued. Eventually a young man came forward who could part-pay the asking price. He was partially disabled and was looking for something interesting to do. The amount that he could afford to pay would just clear the bank overdraft and Jean and I agreed to lend him the rest of the money on the understanding that the loan would be paid off over five years. He was very enthusiastic about running the museum and was full of ideas for its future, so we decided to take his offer and put the house and bookshop up for sale, and also my bungalow next door.

We had several people interested in the purchase of my bungalow and true to the agent's predictions there was a Dutch auction between the prospective purchasers and it was sold to a nurse who was very keen to get it. The shop and house took rather longer to sell, but we eventually found a couple who wanted not only to buy the house but also wanted to continue to run the bookshop.

The purchasers were so pleased that they took us out to dinner that night to celebrate the sale. The man was a man after my own heart and we agreed to complete the sale on the 29th February or 1st March. Because we were leaving the upstairs flat completely furnished, we were able to arrange for our furniture to be moved to the storage depot in Wexford, to be forwarded when we had decided where to live in England. While the solicitors were completing the transfer we found that they were dragging their feet, so the purchaser and I sat one either side of my table with both solicitors on the phone and settled their queries as they made them. When one solicitor made an excuse, we said that's funny we have the other solicitor on the phone who says that the query is settled. In this way we received settlement on 1st March 2000 and were able to sail on the midday ferry from Rosslaire with everything completed.

On our arrival at Fishguard we stayed in a hotel overnight and began our journey to the West Country. We stopped at Hereford for lunch but the traffic was so heavy and the town so busy that we decided not to look at property there. We progressed to Exeter where we stayed overnight at a Travel Lodge. The following morning we went on to Okehampton where some sheltered housing was advertised, but we did not like the site of these. We did however, buy a glass hooker pipe from a charity shop. Eventually, we made our way to Bideford and stayed with Sean and his new partner Sally who had given birth to a little boy – my first grandchild. We had some friends in Appledore who had visited us in Ireland and knew of a cottage to rent for short periods, so we took this while we looked round.

We inspected a lot of properties until we found a two bedroomed house by the river in Bideford in a charming development estate which looked like a Mediterranean fishing village. We went ahead and purchased the house complete with garage, which I turned into a workshop. We had new carpet put down throughout the ground floor of the house. The carpet which was taken up was laid in the garage which made it warmer to work at my bench. I had some metal cupboards fitted which were ideal for sorting most of my tools and equipment for making model boats. The last job was to have electricity laid out to the garage.

As I got older, I found that my paralysis was getting more difficult to control and I needed some form of help. A neighbour at

Riverside had a stairlift and no longer had any use for it. We got in touch with the manufacturer who relocated it for us. This helped enormously for me to get upstairs. I also got a powered armchair which raised me to a standing position and alternatively raised my legs when I wished to relax. I also had a massage unit fitted which certainly helped to loosen my joints up. After a period of much saving, I bought a disability scooter. Actually I bought two scooters, because, when we went to the disability centre in Barnstaple, they told us that there was an offer starting that week for two scooters for the price of one; a road-worthy one and a light fold-down one. This solved the problem of taking a scooter in the car, if we travelled. It proved very useful when we visited Falmouth for a short break. I was able to get round the Maritime Museum, which had recently been opened. I spent the morning in the museum while Jean explored the town. We stayed at a bed and breakfast place which catered for disabled people and had electric plugs suitable for recharging scooters.

As our health had not been too good, we contacted an agency and were lucky enough to be recommended a lovely lady to help us with housework. Over the last few years she has helped us immensely, including two house moves!

We next turned our attention to the garden. On looking around St John's Nursery in Barnstaple, we saw a good lean-to conservatory. We obtained a quotation for it to be fitted on the rear of the house with access through the French doors in the sitting-room. The ground that remained after this had been errected was landscaped by a builder friend from Saltrens and we were very pleased with the result. We were able to get slabs to match the stone circle and coloured bricks, which were discontinued, at a special reduced price and he laid them all with a low brick wall surrounding the circle to make borders outside the circle. We were also able to make an arbour with a wooden arch which was already in the garden and a seat with cupboards on either side, which made a perfect place to rest the coffee cups. We had erected this in a corner of the garden and I smoked my pipes there. I only smoked about an ounce of tobacco a month and usually bought a supply when we went on our cruises. I had been given a meerschaun pipe by Ross, my daughter, which she brought back from a holiday in

Jean in the garden at Riverside, Bideford

Greece. I very much liked the pipe and considered collecting them. On one occasion we visited Turkey which is one of the areas in the world where the pink meerschaum clay is mined. We stayed for Christmas one year and there were two shops devoted to these pipes, so we purchased quite a few. I had also seen some in a tobacconist in Barnstaple. Wherever we travelled, we looked for pipes and I purchased where I could. Jean had bought me some when she was in Scotland, and my collection grew considerably.

About the third year after we had lived in Riverside, Jean had a mild heart attack. It frightened me and I called an ambulance. When they came, after about five minutes, they were very efficient and gave her oxygen and carried her into the ambulance and radioed to the Barnstaple hospital with her details to have a bed prepared and the necessary help to be available. We raced to Barnstaple with sirens going and I sat at the bottom of her stretcher in the back of the ambulance. It was quite an experience for me. Jean settled down but they decided to keep her in overnight so I phoned Sean and he collected me from the hospital. I got a taxi into the hospital next day to see what was happening and Jean had a good night's sleep and was being released as soon as the doctor had seen her. We got a taxi home but she was to rest for several weeks, so I had to do all the shopping.

There was a Safeways not far from where we lived and I was able to go on my scooter. The store sent a member of the staff round with me collecting what was required. At the checkout they packed my purchases into a large bag on the back of my scooter seat and the basket on my handlebars. I found that they were very helpful and I enjoyed shopping like that. I did this for several weeks until Jean was passed by the doctor to drive again.

The only drawback with the little house at Riverside was that we were very close to other people and our front window was overlooked by our neighbours so we decided to look round for a slightly larger house. There were quite a number of new developments about and we eventually found a new estate in the Northam area, half-way between Bideford and Appledore called Kimberly Park. We looked at several houses on this estate and liked them, but thought that we should sell our own house first before committing ourselves to a new property.

The first agent we put the sale of the house with, did not bring a single enquiry so after three months, we changed agents and had a spate of enquiries. One was from a disabled couple who wanted the stairlift left in, but they were unable to sell their own property. Then we had a local lady who wanted to buy for investment, but could not contact her husband who was away and eventually we had a young lady who had two children and whose husband had a business in Bideford. The sale went through within three weeks and we went back to Kimberly Park and found a three bed-roomed house, the sale of which had fallen through three times. Because we could put a deposit down immediately we got a discount of £12,500 on the sale price, which made the property a very attractive proposition. The young lady in the estate office told us that her husband was a tiler and handyman and we got him to tile the kitchen floor and hang all the pictures and mirrors. He had a gadget that could pick out where the pipes and electric cables were embedded in the walls so that we did not drive nails anywhere near the wiring or plumbing. We also had shelves put up where needed and turned the third bedroom into a library, which Jean had always wanted. There was a reasonably sized garden which was turfed. We got a gardener to come in to cut the grass every second week. There was a garage and parking space in the court yard behind the house. This is where I kept my scooter for the time being until I saw a double door shed advertised in one of the super-stores in Barnstaple. We bought this and Sean helped me to erect it in the corner of the back garden. I had to get the back gate widened in order to drive the scooter in safely and realised that the grass became very muddy when the scooter was driven over it several times. We walked around the estate one day and saw someone having a brick drive laid. The contractor's name and tele-phone number were on a board beside the drive, so we rang them up and got a quotation for the back garden to be laid with these bricks, allowing for two flower borders, and we bought a small summer house to be installed in the other corner of the garden. We then got a landscape gardener to plant the borders. He was a man who grew all his trees and plants from special seed and his plants were of very good quality. The garden faced south and the sun shone right into the sitting-room for most of the day, so our final job was to get a sun-awning fitted over the French doors and the back door into the kitchen. All this took some time but I was able to put a bench in the scooter shed and to use the summer house as a smoking room.

Meanwhile, the Model Boat Club which I had joined in Appledore moved their club meeting place from Appledore to Kenwith Castle in Abbotsham which was about two miles south-west of Bideford. This was a lovely residential home for elderly people and had a lake suitable for sailing our model boats on. We were given the use of one of the lounges for our monthly meetings. It also had a bar which was open on a Wednesday for drinks, so our meetings were always on a Wednesday. There were some cottages in the grounds which were let to older people who could look after themselves. One day when we had an open day, we looked round one of the cottages which was awaiting a new tenant. There was a waiting list for applicants but the cottages were very nice and there were alarms if help was required and meals could be supplied if ordered. Jean and I discussed this and talked to Sean who was able to look over the cottage, and we decided to put our names down on the waiting list, not expecting one to become available for some time.

We were very comfortable at Kimberly Park, and liked the house and garden very much but there was always the problem of children playing in the road and balls coming over into the garden and as we were senior citizens, we found this very dificult to cope with. There was a very nice playing field below the estate but when I asked one boy, who was playing outside our front door, why he did not play in the recreation ground, he said that his mother had said that he was not to get his shoes dirty on the grass, but to play on the road!

After being in the house for twelve months we had a letter from Kenwith Castle to say that there was a cottage available if we would like it. Of course, we were off to see it straightaway and liked it very much. We had already enquired about letting our Kimberley Park house on a twelve months lease and realised that the rent which we would receive would offset the rent which we would be paying at Kenwith Castle. The cottage overlooked the lake which was surrounded lovely trees with wild birds on the water.

We put the letting of Kimberly Park in the hands of an agent and tenants were found within three days. They had good references so we arranged the letting and got our friends from Saltrens to move our furniture into the cottage. Of course, moving from a three bedroomed house to a one bedroomed cottage meant that we had to sell some of our surplus furniture and we arranged for some private sales and some went to auction. Sean took my computer and printer for grandson Jack and a friend in Appledore took the bedsitter and several small things so that when the day came for moving, Jean had measured all the wall space in the cottage and made a plan of where everything was to go. Because all the wardrobes in Kimberley Park were built into the walls, we bought a wardrobe flat pack from Argos and got Sean to assemble it. It was quite a hectic day when we moved and we were very tired at the end, but at least we had our bed properly positioned and my electric chair was installed, so we were able to relax in the evening with the television working, thanks again to Sean.

Kenwith Castle and lake

We settled down very well in the cottage and there was a shelter with a charging point for my big scooter and the fold-up one stood in the recess in the entrance hall out of the way. The cottage had the kitchen and sitting-room upstairs, which gave us a lovely view over the lake and the bedroom and bathroom were on the ground floor.

There was a stairlift fitted but it was old and the electric power had been switched off so the battery had deteriorated. I had a new one fitted and it not only took me up the stairs but was useful for anything heavy, including meals if we had them delivered from the castle kitchen; we could order meals whenever we required them and they would be delivered to our cottage. The kitchen staff were very good; they would bring the tray upstairs to the table, or we could have the tray put on the stairlift and get the meal up that way. We tried a three course lunch and were very pleased with it. We washed the crockery up and returned it to the kitchen the next day and we were billed for the meals at the end of each month. Our own kitchen was very adequate. All we had to supply was a washing machine, a fridge and a freezer. We brought the washing machine and freezer from our previous house and bought a new fridge as we had sold our previous fridge-freezer which was too big to fit in. There was a nice electric cooker supplied so we had no trouble cooking our own food, especially since we had brought our own microwave with us. During the time we were in the cottage we changed some of the light fittings and we had a walk-in shower fitted.

It took us some time to settle all the things which we required and there were quite a lot of items which were surplus to our requirements which we either gave away or sold. When at Riverside, I had volunteered to help at the local day centre and I enjoyed this very much and while living there I went on my scooter. When we moved to Kimberley Park, Jean took me for the first few weeks. Then I discovered that Joy, the other volunteer lived in Northam and she offered to collect me on her way and bring me home. I was also lucky with the yacht club as a member came to live just round the corner from where I lived and he took me to the meetings at Kenwith Castle. It all proved very convenient.

The nurse who organised the entertainment at Springfield had an awful time trying to find things for the clients each day. They had about thirty people coming in at about 10.30 am on two mini-buses or taxis. They had coffee or tea at about 11.00 am which on a Wednesday was served by Joy and I. Then the cups had to be collected, the tables cleared and laid for lunch. When this was done, we sold raffle tickets for a draw in the afternoon. Lunch, which was cooked at another council home and delivered at about 12.30 and was served by the nurses for all. When this was completed and coffee served, I dealt with library books and videos for any who required them. We had a good selection of books which were changed every three months and were free to borrow but I had to keep a record of who borrowed them and when they were returned. The videos were charged at 20p per week. The money received from the raffle and the videos went to a fund which provided for expenses on entertainment and Christmas meals. I must say that the nurses did a lot of extra work in supplying things for the entertainment of the clients. There were always prizes required for bingo and cards and other entertainment.

I volunteered to give a talk on pipes and Jean and I brought in our cabinets of carved pipes to illustrate this talk. I also gave a talk on model ship building and brought some of my model ships, especially one which could be taken to pieces, to illustrate the talk. Once I had successfully given talks on a Wednesday, they wanted me to give them on other days. The talks were very welcome because it was very difficult for the nurses to get something different every day.

At the model boat club at Kenwith Castle we had open days twice a year where we gave a display of our models and those which sailed on the lake were scheduled at specific times to give a display which could be seen by the retired inmates from their rooms. There was also a fireworks display in early November and the kitchen sold lovely hot soup and rolls for the visitors. We took advantage of this and held a house-warming party where Sean and I brought some soup and rolls back to the house for our guests.

It was anticipated that we would end our days at the cottage or, if one of us became ill, we could move into the residential home and be looked after. As spring approached, we were able to sit out in the grounds or walk round the lake. I used my scooter to drive by the lake and sit and smoke my pipe and watch the waterfowl. I also took up painting and sat by the lake which gave me plenty of subjects for sketching and painting. Sean and Sally had bought me an easel for my birthday and Jean got me some watercolour paints and a kit from the art and bookshop in Atlantic Village, a shopping centre not far from us. All the while Jean could drive, we had lots of local places that we could visit so that our time was well occupied.

Although I have been disabled since the age of eleven, I feel that I have achieved, perhaps, more things than I could have expected, looking back over the last seventy years since my accident. Jean and I are very content to be settled in such a lovely area after all our experiences in life

Edward Gaskell publishers
DEVON

'. . . that best portion of a good man's life: his little,
nameless, unremembered acts of kindness and love. . .' .

ISBN 189854693-2

Edward Gaskell *publishers*
DEVON